UNCENSORED

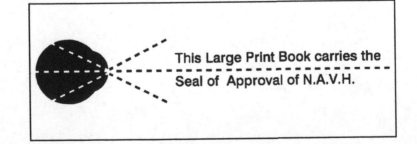

This Large Print Book carries the
Seal of Approval of N.A.V.H.

UNCENSORED

MY LIFE AND UNCOMFORTABLE CONVERSATIONS AT THE INTERSECTION OF BLACK AND WHITE AMERICA

ZACHARY R. WOOD

THORNDIKE PRESS
A part of Gale, a Cengage Company

COOK MEMORIAL LIBRARY
413 N. MILWAUKEE AVE.
LIBERTYVILLE, ILLINOIS 60048

GALE
A Cengage Company

Farmington Hills, Mich • San Francisco • New York • Waterville, Maine
Meriden, Conn • Mason, Ohio • Chicago

GALE
A Cengage Company

LIBRARY OF CONGRESS CIP DATA ON FILE.
CATALOGUING IN PUBLICATION FOR THIS BOOK
IS AVAILABLE FROM THE LIBRARY OF CONGRESS.

ISBN-13: 978-1-4328-5377-8 (hardcover)

Published in 2018 by arrangement with Dutton, an imprint of Penguin
Publishing Group, a division of Penguin Random House, Inc.

Printed in Mexico
1 2 3 4 5 6 7 22 21 20 19 18

*To my sister, whose presence
reminds me of the power of love,
and
to the memory of my grandfather,
who taught me to believe in the
potential of everyone to be
better than they are*

CONTENTS

CONTENTS

AUTHOR'S NOTE

The opportunity to write this book arose while I was attending Columbia University as a visiting student during my junior year of college. Shortly after Thanksgiving, I wrote an article for *The Washington Post* describing the challenges I faced when going home for the holidays as a low-income student. The article gained traction, and I was extremely fortunate to receive an e-mail from Brandi Bowles, who would become my literary agent, who suggested I write a memoir. Before replying, I considered what writing about my life would entail. How would doing so affect my family and my future? After weighing the significant costs and benefits of sharing my story, I gladly accepted the offer to give it a shot.

What I have tried to do is write a memoir that speaks to the truth of how I became who I am. At every turn, that has meant revealing personal information that causes me a great deal of anxiety. I have not taken this approach because I thought people should know painful details of my private life. I've tried within these pages to put myself out there because I've come to believe that one of the best ways to build empathy and compassion is through honesty and vulnerability.

Making this effort hasn't been easy, and throughout the process, I've considered the various risks involved with auto-biographical writing — from misremembering events or details of dialogue to the desire to tailor the narrative in ways that endear the writer. I've tried my best to avoid these hazards.

This book is based on my best recollections of various events in my life. To protect their privacy, I have changed the names and identifying characteristics of some people mentioned in the book. To further disguise the identities of some individuals, certain characters appear as composites of people I've known. In service of the narrative, in a few instances, I have also rearranged and/or compressed events and time periods and re-created dialogue to match my best recollection of past exchanges.

It is my hope that after reading this book, you will come away with the desire to learn more about the experiences and opinions of others — and the determination to use that knowledge to make a positive difference.

If you can talk with crowds and keep your
  virtue,
   Or walk with Kings — nor lose the
   common touch,
If neither foes nor loving friends can hurt
  you,
   If all men count with you, but none too
   much;
If you can fill the unforgiving minute
   With sixty seconds' worth of distance
   run,
Yours is the Earth and everything that's in
  it,
   And — which is more — you'll be a
   Man, my son!
                  — Rudyard Kipling, "If —"

INTRODUCTION

"Do black people come from apes?" a high school friend of mine asked, looking me in the eye. His dad had told him about Charles Murray's book *The Bell Curve*, which links intelligence to race and class in America. "You know, black people are always good at four things," my friend continued, "running, jumping, stealing, and shooting."

At the elite private school I attended, which took two hours to get to by public transportation, I sometimes heard these types of comments. These same students would call the neighborhood I grew up in poor, and though it was dangerous and considered by some to be one of the city's rougher areas, it was where my father worked harder than anyone I'd ever met. So when race came up, either subtly or overtly, his image was the one I carried of my neighborhood and my blackness.

"Zach, why are black people so athletic?"

15

they asked me. Other times, they insisted that I impersonate Obama and complained that my nose wasn't big enough for me to really be black. Did I like this? Of course not. But did it faze me? Please. I had been learning how to adapt to difficult circumstances since before I could remember. Sometimes I debated race with these students; other times it seemed futile. No matter the case, I always tried my best to show through my own actions that the things they believed about black people weren't true. But I knew that I could make a bigger impact by going to the source and learning every facet of their arguments so that I could ultimately take them on. I filed away Charles Murray's name, but not in order to avoid it. Rather, so that I could seek out his books and educate myself about exactly what he was saying, and why.

Only three years later, I had an opportunity to do just that. As the president of Uncomfortable Learning at Williams College, I had the job of bringing speakers who would offer different viewpoints from those we were typically exposed to on our liberal campus. First, I invited Suzanne Venker, a self-described anti-feminist who claims that feminist women are waging a war on men. Within minutes of announcing the event, my in-box, phone, and Facebook page were flooded with negative comments, insults, and even implicit threats. "Zach Wood, you're a filthy misogynist," my peers said. "You're a sellout, a traitor to your race. You're worse than Ben Carson."

I was shocked. Many of these comments were coming from students who knew me. They'd engaged with me on campus, and some were even my friends. Yet, based on this one event, they were characterizing me in a way that went against everything I stood for. But I was determined not to back down. When we eventually had to cancel Venker's appearance due to concerns about her personal safety, I followed up with an invitation to John Derbyshire, a divisive pop-math author and opinion journalist who'd publicly defended white supremacy, advised readers to stay away from groups of black people, and, like Murray, claimed that blacks had lower IQs than whites.

This time, the backlash was even worse. Now the topic was race. A note was slipped under my door that read, "Your blood will be in the leaves," next to a picture of a tree. A comment on Facebook read, "We need the oil and switch to deal with him in this midnight hour." A few student activists came up to me in the cafeteria and insulted me to my face. Others whispered about me behind my back.

I tried explaining to my fellow students that I wasn't doing this because I was secretly a conservative, a self-hating black man, or an anti-feminist, men's rights activist. Rather, I was sick of living in an echo chamber. At Williams, most of my professors taught their perspective on any given issue as if it were fact instead of delving into opposing views to create well-rounded lessons. Around campus, progressive ideas were lauded while conservative ones were shut down for being insensitive. The few conservatives at Williams were largely scared into silence, knowing that if they went against the status quo they would be labeled as biased and wrong.

I wasn't satisfied hearing only one side of things, even if it was the side I agreed with. I wanted to use the education I received at Williams to create positive change in the world one day. How would I do that if I shut out the voices I disagreed with instead of engaging with them? My curiosity led me to examine issues from all sides, trying to find understanding and hopefully some common ground. It wasn't about letting a racist convince me that I was wrong or that I was less intelligent than he was. Instead, I sought to stand firmer in my convictions and become better able to defend them by thoroughly understanding the logic of my opponents.

My explanations made little difference. When the president of Williams College, Adam Falk, canceled Derbyshire's talk, I was disappointed but not deterred. Charles Murray had reached out to me, saying that he'd love to come speak at Williams, and I decided to invite him. While some students continued to protest, this time the event went on as planned.

In his book, Murray attributed IQ disparities and achievement gaps to the genetic inferiority of blacks and the behavioral impediments holding back black communities. One of Murray's contentions was that there are cultural problems in the black community that no amount of welfare or government spending can possibly correct. As he was explaining some of his ideas over dinner, I realized that the IQ discussion was just a distraction. If I focused on the actual issues, maybe we could find some common ground. So I started by acknowledging his side of the argument head-on.

"I am not discounting cultural problems," I told him, going on to describe them better than he could: the emulation of rappers, the

19

glorification of hip-hop culture and violence, the broken families, and so on. "But," I continued, "we need to address the structural issues first. You do acknowledge that they exist, right? So how can we increase social mobility and economic opportunity for Americans living below the poverty line?"

Murray engaged thoughtfully but continued on undeterred. After the event, a friend approached me to say that my argument had resonated with him and had even made him think differently about racial disparities in America. For me, Murray's visit to Williams was a successful example of Uncomfortable Learning. Neither of us changed our opinions or switched sides, but that wasn't the point. Instead, by listening to and challenging Murray, my classmates and I were forced to think more deeply about our own beliefs and even question them.

In my mind, this type of debate is valuable and would not have been possible if we did not give Murray an opportunity to share his perspective, but my critics felt that by giving him that opportunity, I was bolstering his misguided and often hurtful views.

Hurtful. That's the word that campus activists and others who opposed Murray's invitation to speak at Williams used to describe why they were against it. As I sat down with some of them to hear them out, just as I'd heard out Murray, they explained why it was so painful and triggering for them. They discussed incidents of sexual assault, police brutality, and growing up in poverty, and they explained that, to them, Williams wasn't just a learning institution — it was their home.

As the topic of free speech on college campuses has continued to cause controversy, protests, and even bursts of violence across the country, the criticism most often levied against campus activists is that they're too sensitive. On campus, their feelings are coddled. Class materials that may be upsetting are given a trigger warning. Speech codes restrict many college students from talking about certain subjects. And controversial speakers such as Venker and Derbyshire are kept away. The result is millions of college students who have little tolerance for healthy debate and view someone voicing his or her opposing view as an attack on their very personhood.

Make no mistake — these subjects are extremely difficult for me to grapple with, too. But I don't want to give someone like Derbyshire the satisfaction of writing me off as too sensitive when I can rise to the occasion and challenge him instead.

And, yes, of course there's more to it than that. This is something I've been asked about many times. In several of the interviews I've done following the Uncomfortable Learning controversy, I've been asked why my peers are so sensitive and what makes me different.

"Your classmates are hurt by someone like Murray merely being on campus, and you're willing to face implicit threats in order to bring him there," one reporter remarked during a phone interview. "How have you grown such a thick skin? Are you just wired differently than the students who criticize you?"

I repeated the question, trying to think of how best to answer. This was something I'd been asked many times, but not in such a pointed way. The truth is, I know full well where my thick skin comes from. It's something I've processed and moved on from, but once in a while when I'm asked a question like this, I think back to her words: "You worthless punk-ass nigga." I can remember the piercing look in her eyes, the leather belt in her hand, the anger and pain that made her face quiver as she told me to take off my clothes and turn around.

"Well," I said slowly, taking a deep breath. "I wasn't exactly coddled."

CHAPTER 1
CROSSROADS

My mother was the first person I desperately tried to understand. She was five feet seven with mahogany skin and a beautiful smile. She was born in Fort Worth, Texas, but spent most of her childhood in Detroit. She was a people person, with excellent soft skills, and she rarely made anything less than a great first impression when she wanted to.

But I could never take her words at face value. When I was about four years old she sat me down and told me in graphic detail what my father had done that forced her to leave him. She sat, unblinking, her face mere inches from mine. "Your father," she said slowly through clenched teeth, drawing each word out as she gestured with the lit cigarette that dangled from between her fingers, "took me by my shoulders and threw me down on the ground. He pinned me there, Zachary," she continued, "calling me a fucking bitch and holding me down with all his strength until I could hardly breathe."

I was terrified. I didn't want to hear any more, but even at the age of four I knew better than to interrupt my mother when she was speaking. "Then he picked me up," she said, her brow knit and eyes focused, "and threw me against the wall. It hurt to walk, but I ran into your room to get you so that we could leave. But your father blocked the doorway and refused to let us out."

I was later told that when my father left for work the next morning, my mother borrowed money from a friend to rent an apartment, and the two of us moved out of our house in Forestville, Maryland. For weeks, my dad had no idea where my mom and I were. During that time, she filled my head with lies about my father, repeating this violent, graphic story over and over with her voice and eyes full of fear and anger.

I had nightmares about my father knocking my mom over, slapping her, and throwing her to the ground. But had he done those things? My young mind was confused. The details of his beatings were there in my memory, but they didn't feel the same as other memories that I knew to be true. I couldn't tell what was real.

Finally, my mom's mom, whom I called Lola, convinced my mother to let me see my father again. I was so happy to be back home at his house, but I was also confused. All weekend, I wouldn't stop asking my father questions about what had happened between him and my mom. "Daddy, did you hurt Mommy? Did you hit her?"

"No," he said with a sigh. "That's not how I remember it." He never said she was lying. But I sensed from spending time with my father that her stories were biased. I loved being with my dad. He was at work a lot, but when he got home he'd throw some meat and vegetables into the oven and take me to the park to play. My dad has always been a gym rat. He's in great shape to this day, and when I was a kid he had at least as much energy as I did. And I always had a lot of energy.

This was how my dad showed his affection — by doing rather than saying. He was emotionally reserved but engaged, a man of few words. He rarely told me that he loved me, but he showed me clearly that he did by always being there, ready to play with me and make his best efforts at answering my endless questions. No matter how exhausted or frustrated he was, he never raised his voice. His house, which I still thought of as home, was a place of peace.

It was in direct contrast to life with my mom, and I missed my dad terribly when he wasn't around. A few months after we'd moved out of my dad's house, we were going through a drive-through when I told my mom, "I want to be with my dad."

Now, this memory is crystal clear. My mom took the bag of food and sped off, abruptly stopping the car a few yards away. She reached over to the passenger seat, grabbed me, and forcefully placed me in her lap. She put her hands on my shoulders and began shaking me aggressively.

"No, Zachary," she said over and over as she shook me. "No, no, no, no, no." I felt dizzy. "Tell me you love me." She kept on shaking me. My head was spinning. "Tell me that you want to live with me." I just cried. I was so scared. I had never seen her that angry. "Tell me, Zachary."

"Yes," I finally said in a small voice, and she abruptly stopped. I was still crying, and my head hurt, but she placed me back in my seat and drove off as if nothing had happened. I didn't say a word for the rest of the day.

When I think about these early memories, I try to reconcile them with the many times my mom said, "If you fail at raising your

children, nothing else in life really matters."
It was a paraphrase of her favorite quotation from Jacqueline Kennedy, whom she admired for her elegance and sophistication. When I think about the fear and pain I felt as a child, I try to remember the amazing birthday parties my mother threw for me and the times she sat me down one-on-one and said, "Zachary, I love you more than you will ever know. Honey, I love you more than life itself."

Even when I resented her for how she made me feel, I loved my mother dearly, just as I do now. As I look back, it's easier to see how as a little kid my mind was overwhelmed by the expectation of her rage. Though I never doubted that she loved me, the abuse I endured often made it difficult for me to feel her love.

Different people yell at varying levels of intensity — a raised voice, a shout, a quick holler. When my mother yelled, it was as if all her rage were being unleashed — and she had a lot of rage. She yelled with high intensity for as long as she could. Many times, she'd scream at me until her voice became hoarse. Then she'd take a break and start yelling again when her voice returned.

While she was yelling, I had to stand up straight and still and maintain eye contact with her the entire time. If I slouched or dropped my gaze, it would make things worse. Sometimes she'd yell while sitting back in her chair, smoking a cigarette. But most of the time, she would stand uncomfortably close to me, staring me right in the eyes. If I wasn't focusing enough on what she was saying, she'd point her finger right up to my eye, so close that it was almost touching. "Don't blink," she said sternly. "Don't you fucking blink."

I always looked forward to visits with my dad, but they were never frequent enough for me. The second-best thing was trips to see my grandma Lola and her husband, whom I called Papa, in Detroit. They were both retired, so they spent all their time with me when I visited. Lola had been an elementary school teacher for more than twenty years in the Detroit public school system, and Papa was a child psychologist.

Shortly after my third birthday, I went to stay with Lola and Papa for four weeks, and Lola taught me to read. I loved it, sitting there on her lap, watching her trace each word on the page with three fingers as she read to me.

Lola showered me with gifts and special treats. She promised that if I worked with her on my reading every morning, she would take me to Crossroads. Crossroads was short for Great Lakes Crossing Outlets mall. As a little kid, I thought it was absolutely the coolest place in the world. It was so big and was filled with a dizzying number of colors, contraptions, and curiosities. The mall had a Rainforest Cafe, with a life-size mechanical alligator that rose out of the water and snapped its jaws when I walked up close to it. I was tempted to run up and smack it and then run away before it could bite me. I did this over and over again.

Crossroads also had the largest, most colorful, and most inviting play area I'd ever seen. Instead of a standard jungle gym, there were huge fruits and vegetables the size of SUVs made of glazed rubber for kids to climb, jump, and slide on. After I finished my reading, Lola took me to the mall and sat there watching me while I played. After I had spent all my energy, we got Bourbon chicken from our favorite place in the food court.

It took an hour to get to Crossroads from Lola's house, and during those rides back and forth she told me all about the trips she'd taken with Papa to western Europe, China, Japan, Russia, and South America. She explained to me that in different cultures, people valued different things, and

31

that we shouldn't assume things about people until we understood their backgrounds. I rested my head on the car window, tired out from the long day of playing, and imagined the faces of the people who lived in these foreign countries. How were their lives similar to mine? I wondered. How were they different?

When I got back to DC after visiting Lola and Papa, my mom had a new boyfriend, Kevin. He was born and raised in Virginia. He was a relatively quiet man — dark skinned, short, and stocky, with a strong work ethic. Kevin had a bald head and pimples that must have been with him since puberty. He was hard of hearing and tried to keep to himself, but my mom was always picking a fight with him. She made Kevin sleep in the basement and frequently told him he wasn't a real man. For some reason he worshipped her and would do whatever she asked, whether it was to tell me bad things about my father, slash her boss's tires, or beat up another guy who looked at her the wrong way. I was a child; I was completely dependent on my mom, and she made me believe that I would never be able to survive without her. But, hard as I tried, I never understood why Kevin stayed.

Kevin had a nephew named Warren who was around my age and often played at our house. One day when I was about five years old, Warren dared me to draw on the wall, and I did it. Of course, Warren immediately tattled to Kevin, who told my mom. After sending Kevin to take Warren home, she calmly told me, "Go get the flyswatter and take off your clothes."

Slowly, reluctantly, I did as she said. When I came back into the room, she pointed her finger right up to my eye. "You better not drop a fucking tear," she said before turning me around. I braced myself for what I knew was coming. Pow. Pow. Pow. This went on for several minutes, until my whole backside was stinging. Then she stopped. She ordered me into her bedroom, turned off all the lights, and slammed the door closed.

Alone in the dark, I cried. I was afraid to lie on her bed, so I lay on the floor for hours. My mom came back into the room after midnight and started yelling. For hours, she told me what a disappointment I was, how ungrateful I was, how I didn't love her enough, and that I was just like my father.

It always went back to my father. Even in her calmer moments, she was fixated on my dad. She desperately wanted me to hate him, or to at least pretend that I did. She told me that if ever he took me away from her, she and Kevin would hang my father upside down and use a potato peeler to castrate him.

On nights like these, I went to bed wishing that I'd never wake up. I was too young to have any real understanding of death. I just wanted the pain to end. If she was this mad at me, I reasoned, then I must have been fundamentally bad, and maybe God was mad at me, too. I was afraid that if I did die, I'd go to hell, but I wasn't sure it would be much worse.

Early the next morning, my mom ran into my room and flipped on the lights singing the *Green Acres* theme song by Vic Mizzy at the top of her lungs.

"Mommy, I'm tired," I told her. I had barely slept the night before.

"Come on, buddy, wake up," she responded with a wide smile. "Sweet pea, Mama's pooh bear, a ziggity Zach — a Zach attack, sing it with me."

I closed my eyes, too exhausted to join in the fun. I knew that she wouldn't stop until I rolled over, gave her a kiss, and climbed out of bed. On days like this, instead of being angry or sad, she was full of energy and ready to have fun. These were the days I most looked forward to. My mom took me out to breakfast at Denny's or Bob Evans, and then we went to Chuck E. Cheese's and played arcade games for hours. She didn't just watch me play like the other moms. No, she was so into the experience that she even climbed around in the Sky Tubes, jumped in the ball pit, and went through the fun house with me. But our favorite game was Skee-Ball. We competed to see who could get the highest score, laughing and talking smack as we tried to outdo each other. But most of the time, she ended up letting me win.

After spending several hours at Chuck E. Cheese's, my mom took me to the movies. We paid for two tickets to whatever kids' movie was playing and then snuck into a second movie after that one ended. It was still daylight out after the second movie, so we went go-cart racing. My mom loved the go-carts. My feet didn't yet reach the pedals, so I just sat beside her as she drove, hooting and laughing the entire time.

After that, she let me choose where to go for dinner. I picked Famous Dave's, because they had the best barbecue in town. But my mom wasn't satisfied with the options offered in a single meal, so she ordered several large platters, far more than the two of us could possibly eat. Our last stop before heading home was at Baskin-Robbins for ice cream. I was completely stuffed, but I made sure to eat my ice cream, not wanting for a moment to seem ungrateful.

While my mom's moods and behavior were completely unpredictable, I could count on having a day like this at least once every couple of weeks. The itinerary varied a bit, but for the most part it remained similar. I suffered through a beating or tirade about once a week, but every so often I was pleasantly surprised. My mom would go several consecutive days craving thrills and recreation without any mood swings. But some surprises were less pleasant. Shortly after divorcing my dad, Mom moved us to Michigan to be closer to Lola and Papa. Then she and Lola got into a big fight, so we moved back to DC. Over the next few years we moved back and forth from Michigan to the DC area three more times.

By the time I started first grade we were back in Detroit. I spent a lot of time at Lola and Papa's house. I loved playing in their basement, which was filled with action figures and books. My favorite action figures were WWE wrestlers, Hulk Hogan and the Rock. My favorite books back then were by

Shel Silverstein. I read *The Giving Tree* so many times that before long I had it memorized. There was something about the story of unconditional love and giving that resonated with me.

But the first book that changed the course of my life was a biography of Albert Einstein that I found in an old, forgotten box of books. The name of the author was faded with age, and the dust jacket was torn, but I had never been so interested in a book before. I remember being fascinated by the fact that Einstein didn't just study his one area of expertise; he loved knowledge, literature, and asking philosophical questions about the world. He wanted to learn and know as much as possible.

Reading about someone with a great mind who was able to do amazing things with it taught me that there was more to life than I'd ever previously imagined. Life wasn't just about doing and experiencing things. An entirely different type of life existed: the life of the mind. Using the mind, anything was possible. I could transcend my own reality and gain a deep knowledge about things without having experienced them; I could see the world from the eyes of someone I'd never even met and use my imagination to stretch myself, grow, and understand.

I started to read anything and everything I could get my hands on. Luckily, my mom's house, as well as Lola's, was filled with books. My mom graduated from the University of Maryland and then earned her master's degree in social justice from Marygrove College in 2007. She even pursued a PhD in behavioral health and completed all the necessary course work except for a final dissertation. She had always enjoyed reading. She stored about fifty books on a top shelf in the closet in my bedroom, high above my reach. I pulled a chair over to the closet and stood on my tiptoes to get the books down. Over the next few months, I read them all and marked the words I couldn't pronounce so that I could look them up later. It was hard to understand some of the passages, but I liked the challenge of rereading sentences and seeing how much I could infer about the meaning of words from their context.

Now that I was in school, my mom saved most of her fun-filled days for the weekends or days off. But on several occasions, she called the school and simply told them I was sick. Then she'd hang up the phone and tell me, "Well, buddy, it's time to play hooky!" The first time she did this, I asked her what "hooky" meant. After explaining that it was a day off from school or work for play, she told me that we'd watch *Ferris Bueller's Day Off* later that evening. It was one of her favorite movies.

When I wasn't wishing I'd never wake up, I went to sleep hoping that the next day my mom would wake up and want to have fun, because I dreaded being around her when she was angry. I never knew what was coming next. Every morning when I woke up, I had to quickly read all the signs to surmise what kind of mood she was in and act accordingly. On good days, her behavior was lighthearted, playful, and energetic. On bad days, she was severely distressed, and I worried about her. It was clear that she was suffering. She believed that every color she saw held a secret message and dragged me along, chasing buses and trucks, reading them for a sign that would tell her what to do next.

I was still in the first grade when my mom started to believe that the government was after her. She was certain that she was being followed and our house was bugged. For months, I wasn't allowed to speak to her inside our house or in public. If I wanted to say anything, I had to write it down on a piece of paper. A few times, I slipped up and accidentally spoke, and she blew up at me.

"You ungrateful little bitch-ass nigga," she told me through gritted teeth after she'd worn herself out from yelling. "You won't be living in this house much longer if you don't do what I say. I'll put you in a nice little box, tape it up, and send your ass to Afghanistan. Don't fuck with me, Zachary."

The war had just begun in Afghanistan, and the news each night was filled with horrifying scenes from the front lines. I was so young and terrified that I didn't know any better than to believe her. "Look me in the eye," she commanded, pointing her finger directly at my retina. "Say, 'I love you, Mommy.' "

"I love you," I muttered, fighting back tears.

"Huh," she said, temporarily satisfied, as she took a drag from her cigarette. "You better appreciate all I do for you, or your black ass will wake up in Afghanistan."

I wanted to confide in someone about what was going on at home, but I was too afraid. My mom told me repeatedly that if I ever said anything bad about her to my dad, Kevin would "fuck him up." So I covered up by always acting happy and content. I must have done a good job, because no one suspected a thing — not my dad, and not even Papa, who had been a child psychologist.

Looking back, though, I can see that there may have been some signs of trouble. When I visited my dad, he noticed that I didn't play with my toys. Instead, I used other, bigger toys and objects I found around the house to destroy them. I used all my strength to rip my action figures apart, limb from limb. I snapped my dad's high school basketball trophies in half, smashed my toy trucks into LEGO towers, and rammed them into the wall until various parts fell off. Once, I even found a sledgehammer in the closet and smashed my toy cash register with it over and over until my dad ran over and took away the hammer. No one ever asked why I was doing this, but I remember it feeling almost cathartic, a way of letting out the anger and frustration I'd tucked away.

After my mom threatened to send me to Afghanistan, I did finally confide in my grandmother. I was too afraid to tell her everything, but I talked to her about my mom's paranoia. I told Lola that I loved my mom, that it made me feel good to see her happy — laughing and smiling — but most of the time she was either really angry or really sad. Though I felt powerless to help my mom, I also felt that I would have been a better son if I could make her life easier. A better son would have given his mother fewer reasons to be mad at him and more reasons to be proud of him. This desire to help, to do more, and to be of greater value stuck with me but would later factor into the worst mistake I've ever made.

After I talked to Lola, she encouraged my mom to check herself into a psychiatric hospital, and for four blessed months I was free. I stayed with Lola and Papa and visited my mom in the hospital once a week. Lola explained to me that my mother was going through a hard time and that she was getting help so that she could be there for me.

Every time I walked into my mom's hospital room, her face crumbled. "Come here, Zachary," she said, her eyes filling with tears as she reached forward to give me a big hug. After asking me about school and what I'd been up to, she veered into a strange conversation about an old man in the hospital named Silas who always asked her to buy him ice cream and why she thought the government wanted to turn her into a lesbian.

Back at Lola and Papa's house, books

became my refuge. The only thing I didn't like about staying there was that I had to go to bed earlier than I did with my mom, so I hid a flashlight under my covers and stayed up reading after Lola thought I was asleep. In the basement, I found a collection of slim volumes about black historical figures. There were biographies about the inventor Garrett Morgan, George Washington Carver, Harriet Tubman, Frederick Douglass, Rosa Parks, W. E. B. DuBois, and so many more. There were about forty of these books in all. I spent an entire weekend down in the basement reading them, fascinated to imagine what life must have been like for these people, and all that had transpired since the time when they were alive for things to get to the way they were now.

"What are you doing down there?" Lola asked when she called me upstairs to eat.

"Just playing," I said, shrugging my shoulders. I quickly finished my meal so that I could get back to the books.

But later that night, I couldn't sleep. Something I'd read in the book about Frederick Douglass was bothering me. When Papa came into my room to check on me, I asked, "Why weren't slaves allowed to read?" I had just discovered the way that reading expanded my mind. The idea that it had been illegal for an entire group of people to do so was unfathomable to me.

Papa sat quietly at the foot of my bed for a moment. He had a deep, booming voice, and when he spoke, he did so slowly and deliberately. "Z-Man," he finally said, using one of his nicknames for me, "this country has never been ready for a black man with too much power." He paused before continuing. "The two worst things you can be in this world are black and poor."

At that point, I'd overheard enough grown-up conversations and news reports to know what racism was. Reading about the historical black figures had given me a greater understanding of how African Americans had been disenfranchised throughout history. But this was the first time that someone I cared about and trusted told me point-blank how unfortunate a position I had been born into. It was even more revealing that he was equating the ability to read with power. In those two sentences, Papa had managed to say so much. While we weren't exactly poor — my dad always paid his child support, and Lola and Papa were solidly middle-class — it was clear to me that I didn't have the same types of advantages as someone who'd simply been born into a different situation.

That night I went to sleep thinking about the many obstacles that went along with being black and struggling financially in America. The next morning at breakfast, I told Lola that I wanted to be like Martin Luther King Jr. one day — someone people could look up to and depend on.

Maybe a week later I was on the carpet at school during playtime when I asked the little blond girl next to me if I could share her toy. "No," she told me stubbornly, "it's mine." We had a small childish argument over the toy before she turned to me and taunted, "At least my grandparents weren't slaves."

I was shocked, and I immediately thought back to what Papa had told me just a few days before. He was right, I realized. Slaves were the epitome of being black and poor, and here I was, a direct descendant. I thought about all forty of those books I had read, spanning the past two centuries. So much had transpired and yet so little had actually changed. I was free. I was allegedly equal. And yet this little girl still felt that she had power over me. There I was: still black, maybe not poor, but still disadvantaged — still the two very worst things that I could be.

As my love of books took off, so did my

reading level. Papa gave me a pocket dictionary to use while I was reading, and every time I encountered a new word, I stopped and looked it up. I was still in first grade, but I was reading at a fifth-grade level. The older kids were in a separate building at the school, so I had to put on my coat and leave my class to go over there each day for reading.

The public school I went to wasn't the worst in Detroit, but it wasn't great, either. We didn't have a library at the school, and most of the kids didn't have access to books at home, as I did. It was obvious that many of the other kids there were bright, but they had a lot of problems at home. They often came to school without having eaten and wearing the same dirty clothes from the day before. Those kids would routinely get into fights and would occasionally pick on me for being a good student. My teachers worked hard, but they always seemed exhausted. They discouraged us from asking questions and probing different subjects. It was obvious to me even at that young age that they just wanted to get through the day and go home.

Every time one of my teachers rushed through a lesson or ignored one of my questions, I thought back to what Papa had told me. Most of the kids in my school were black. Yes, we were being taught to read, but we still weren't being taught to think critically or creatively or in any way that would allow us to expand our minds. We were not being given too much power.

After four months, my mom was released from the hospital. She sat me down and told me in a sweet baby voice, "Zachary, honey, Mommy has something called bipolar disorder. It means that how I'm feeling will change, and I don't have control over it. I don't know how I'll feel tomorrow or next week, but just know that I love you more than a monkey loves bananas." She leaned forward and pinched my cheeks, and then her voice grew serious. "I'm going to take my medicine, and I'm going to get better, Zachary," she told me. As I listened to her, I was convinced she meant every word, and I have no doubt that, in that moment, she did. But her behavior had always been unpredictable; the idea that her mind was sick and that she had little control over it was scary and very sad to me.

After that, my mom did stop thinking the government was after her, but everything else went back to our broken version of normal. Some days were filled with terror while others were nonstop fun. When she wasn't angry or seeking thrills, she was usually very depressed and would lie in bed crying, asking me repeatedly if I loved her. I always said yes, even if I was still upset over how she'd treated me the day before. But if I had those moments to do over again, I'd put my emotions aside, give her a hug and a kiss, and try to show more affection.

Most of the time, I was pretty sure she wasn't taking her meds. One day, a few weeks after she got home, I asked her if she'd taken her medicine, as she'd promised. "Zachary, I wiped your black ass when you were little," she told me angrily. "Don't you dare tell me what to do."

Despite what she said, not long after that I began to gain a better understanding of how much control my mom actually did have over some of her behavior. She could stop in the middle of one of her rants, pick up the phone, and thoroughly impress whomever she was speaking to, only to resume yelling the minute she hung up. She would also pull me aside and say, "Watch me fuck with Kevin. I'm gonna get him," and then she would proceed to tell him what a huge disappointment he was, verbally emasculating him until he was literally in tears. Seeing Kevin cry proved to me how difficult life with my mom could be. I already knew that my mom's behavior wasn't normal — and now I had a name for it, bipolar — but it was shocking to see her deliberately reduce a grown man to tears.

This made it even harder for me to receive my mom's love, to reciprocate her affection, or even to entertain the idea of having fun with her like I did when I was little. We still had a lot of fun together sometimes, but I didn't look forward to spending time with her as much as I used to. I usually wanted to stay in my room, away from her, and read or play video games. She was fine with my love of books, but only if it didn't detract from the attention I paid to her. If I spent an hour in my room reading, I had to spend an hour cuddling on the couch with her. Most of the time, I played along to avoid upsetting her — to keep the peace for as long as I could.

But my mom did a lot of good things for me, too. And I know full well that I wouldn't be where I am today without her. She was determined to teach me from a very young age how to present myself well and win people over. She would spend hours coaching me on how to shake someone's hand, introduce myself, look people in the eyes, and hold a conversation. I'd often practice on Lola or Kevin as my mom critiqued my performance. Pretty soon, most people I met immediately commented on what a firm handshake I had and how well-spoken I was. My mom loved getting these compliments and beamed with pride. But on the occasions when I failed to deliver in some small way, I was punished for it later.

During this time, I didn't see my dad as often as he or I would have liked because he was so far away in DC. My mom wasn't about to spend her time driving me down there to see him, and I was too young to fly alone. (Plus it was too expensive.) My dad made the nine-hour drive to see me as often as he could, usually at least once every few months. He'd leave DC right after he got off from work and drive all night, arriving exhausted in the morning to find me excited to see him and full of energy.

"Dad! What are we going to do today?" I'd ask him. It wasn't until years later that I realized how hard this must have been on him. He never let on. Instead of insisting on resting for a bit, he always gathered his energy and took me out to eat or wherever I most wanted to go.

During the summers, I often went to DC to stay with him for a month or even longer. Although my mom would never drive me all the way down to DC, she did let me spend some of each summer with my dad. The summer when I was eight, I went for a special visit. My sister, Nicole, was born. My dad had been dating her mom, Brenda, for a while, and now that they had a child, they moved in together to an apartment in Alexandria, Virginia.

I was so excited to have a sister and to see her for the first time. I wanted to hold her and take care of her, but my dad explained how fragile babies are. He placed Nicole in my arms with his hands securely over her, and I marveled at her tiny features, thrilled to be biologically connected to this pure, brand-new human.

When I wasn't playing with the baby, I spent time reading and playing basketball with my dad. I loved being with him, and I always struggled with the idea that my mom so desperately wanted me to hate him. That was just impossible for me. He was the best father I could have asked for. I could tell him anything, but the one thing I couldn't talk to him about was my mom. One day we were playing basketball at a nearby park when I tried to broach the subject. "Mom gets really mad sometimes," I said.

My dad just shook his head. "Your mom loves you," he told me as he shot the ball, easily swishing it through the net. "She just doesn't know how to express it." I didn't respond. A huge part of me wished that my dad would intuit what I was going through and do something to change it, but it was clear from his demeanor that this conversation was over. And I was too afraid to offer any more detail on my own.

When I got back home to Detroit, my mom insisted on hearing every detail of my visit — what we did, what we ate, every word my dad said. But mostly, she wanted to talk about Brenda. I stood in our living room as she leaned back in her chair and grilled me. "What does her face look like?" she asked me. "What about her hair?"

"I don't know, Mom," I said uncomfortably. At the age of eight, my descriptive powers weren't all that well developed. Plus, I had a feeling that there was no correct way to answer these questions.

"Zachary, I asked you what she looked like," she said, leaning forward in her chair. "You answer me, boy, or I'll take off my belt. Don't make me have to ask you again. I'll knock your goddamn head through the back window."

Nervously, I searched my mind for a way to describe Brenda to my mom. We'd recently watched a Jennifer Lopez movie together, and there might have been a slight resemblance between her and Brenda. "She kinda looks like Jennifer Lopez," I said. And she didn't even really look like Lopez, but I knew who Jennifer Lopez was from watching *Maid in Manhattan,* and so hers was the first woman's name I thought of. Not that Brenda wasn't attractive, but she wasn't Puerto Rican and didn't have straight hair. She actually looks more like Nia Long. That didn't matter, though. Before I even finished my sentence, I realized that I had said the wrong thing. My mother put down her cigarette and leaned forward in her chair. "You think she's more attractive than me," she said. It was a statement, not a question. "You're ashamed of me."

This was the beginning of a three-hour rant about how Brenda was a nasty, dirty-ass ho, my father wasn't a real man, and I was an ungrateful little punk-ass nigga. I just stood there as still as I could, trying my best to maintain eye contact with her the entire time. Every time my posture slumped or my gaze wavered, she threatened to hit me or have Kevin lay his hands on me.

When my mom finally released me, I went to my room. I was so angry and scared that I was shaking, but I didn't want to give her the satisfaction of hearing me cry. At times like these, I turned to the books in my

53

closet. There was one about the Supreme Court that I'd already read several times. I took it off the shelf now and read it again, losing myself in the names of the justices from the last fifty years. Instead of thinking about my mom, I thought about those justices — how they had listened to both sides of an argument and formulated a compelling opinion. This was my escape, a way of thinking myself out of my current situation and into a whole other world.

I preferred that world, so I tried to stay there as long as I could. Even when I was in school, I was always asking questions and trying to learn more. When I saw how this paid off in the form of good grades and praise from my teachers, I was hooked. I realized that if I studied hard, which I enjoyed, I could fill my life outside of home with consistently positive things. So that's what I did.

Over the next few years, I got all A's, and I won several spelling bees and science fairs. Papa encouraged my studies, rewarding me with an allowance when I won a spelling bee or did extra reading. He used these rewards to teach me about money — how to save and invest and resist the temptation to spend it all at once.

The school offered me the opportunity to

skip a grade, based on my standardized test scores, but my dad was against the idea because he wanted me to stay socially normal. I already stood out and got picked on at times for being a good, ambitious student in a culture where it wasn't valued, and he was worried that if I moved up and became the smallest kid in the grade, I'd become a target.

It wasn't until I was in fourth grade that my probing and questioning became a problem. I was still getting great grades, but my teacher wrote on my report card that I was disrupting the class by asking so many questions and at times even challenging what was being taught, alluding to the books I'd read outside of school.

This infuriated my mom. No matter what she may have said to me at home, she was not going to tolerate a teacher reading my intelligence and probing questions as disruptive. "That's it," she told me after reading my report card. "You're done with that school. Those little white boys in Grosse Pointe get the best education, and that's where you're going to go, too."

My mom cared deeply about my education, both at school and in life. By this point, she'd already taught me to swim and then enrolled me in swimming lessons. She thought it was important for me to defy the stereotypes about black people. Soon after, I started taking golf lessons. It was clear that she wanted to do whatever she could to give me as many opportunities as possible. Now she set her sights on Grosse Pointe.

Grosse Pointe was a small, wealthy suburban town. It was adjacent to Detroit, but it might as well have been on another planet, considering the part of town we lived in. Our neighborhood was relatively safe, but I knew there was one direction in which I could not ride my bike. It was the sort of neighborhood where people looked out for one another, yet petty crimes happened all the time. My mom's car was put up on blocks twice, and groups of kids fought in the street from time to time. Our home was a small condo, nothing at all like the huge waterfront mansions in Grosse Pointe.

The Gross Pointe Academy (GPA) was considered the best of the best private schools in the area, with a huge, beautiful campus and a focus on the arts, public speaking, and intellectual development. My mom guided me through the application and interview process, and when I got into the Grosse Pointe Academy, she was determined that a lack of funds wouldn't keep me from going.

My scholarship covered only 90 percent of the tuition, but my dad agreed to make up the difference. It would be a huge strain on his finances, but he wanted to contribute to my education and my future in any way he could. His marriage to my mom hadn't gone the way he'd wanted it to. With my mom and me so far away in Michigan, he couldn't be the type of father that he wanted to be, one who was physically present every day. But no matter how hard it may have been on him, sending me to Grosse Pointe Academy was something he could do.

Of course, I was too young to understand all this at the time. What I knew was that I was going to a new school, one that was known to value learning and curiosity as much as I did. I had no idea that it would challenge me to see myself, my family, and my entire world from a whole new perspective.

CHAPTER 2
DADS' DAY

Right before I started at Grosse Pointe Academy, my mom went back to the hospital. I was getting bigger, and my mom must have sensed that I was growing more aware of the world around me. She knew that if she continued to hurt me physically, I would remember it and eventually tell someone. So she stopped. Just like that. It was a relief, but it was also jarring to me because it was another sign that she could control her actions — at least to some extent. And even though the beatings stopped, her behavior was still disturbing and in many respects became more manipulative.

When she was mad at me now, instead of getting the flyswatter or a leather belt, she set about humiliating me. She would take me to the mall and deliberately make a scene or make me go up to groups of older girls and say ridiculous things. Other times, she would take me to a basketball court in a

rough area and make me tell the guys waiting to play in the next pickup game that I
was soft and afraid to play ball in the hood.
Most of this happened under the threat of
either violence or cruel and unusual punish-
ments. She would say that if I didn't do
what she said, Kevin would put me in my
place when he got home that night, or that
she'd make me dress up like Steve Urkel
and drop me off in a dangerous part of the
city. Either way, I knew that my mom would
make me pay for disobeying her. So I always
tried to comply.

About half the time, after embarrassing
me in public, she would apologize and tell
me how much she loved me. Sometimes she
would even offer to buy me things or take
me out shopping the next day. I usually accepted the apology — to avoid making
things worse — but I rarely expressed much
interest in shopping with her or letting her
buy me something to make up for what she
did.

She was hard on Kevin, too. After they
got into a huge fight and my mom forced
him to sleep in his truck for a week, he
threatened to leave her. It wasn't the first
time; their relationship had always been
contentious. But this time when Kevin came
back he negotiated terms with my mom. If

he was going to stay, she had to let him sleep in her room — though still on the floor — and agree to marry him at some point down the road.

When I confided in Lola about how uncomfortable some of my mother's behavior made me, she looked as if she was going to cry. "Zachary," she told me, "you are a smart, handsome young man. You'll be very successful in life. Don't worry about any of that. Your mom is just crazy."

The pressure from Lola and Kevin convinced my mom to go back to the hospital, this time as a participant in a mental health study. She was gone for only a few days, so I stayed at home with Kevin while a team of psychiatrists discovered that my mom had initially been misdiagnosed as bipolar. Her new diagnosis was schizoaffective disorder, which includes symptoms of both schizophrenia and bipolar disorder. Her doctors tried one medication after another, but nothing seemed to work. She continued in therapy, but she put on a show for her psychiatrists so that they would think she was better. She even began speaking at conferences about the importance of mental health support. They presented her as a success story, as someone who was in full recovery from her illness.

She was not recovered. In some ways, she was worse. My mom had always enjoyed gambling at the casino, but it was around this time that it became an obsession, likely an addiction. She started going to the casino every weekend, and then every night. Most of the time she'd stay out all night, arriving home just in time to take me to school in the morning. Sometimes Kevin was at home, but he worked late shifts and overtime a few days a week, so I was often alone. In some ways, it was a relief not to have her around, but I was scared to be alone in the house late at night. While the block we lived on was not as dangerous as some of the others nearby, there had been several burglaries in the neighborhood since we had moved in. And our house had even been robbed once.

The main thing about all that gambling, though, was that of course my mom needed money. This became her main fixation. She spent my dad's child support and her own salary at the casino, maxed out her credit cards and took out additional loans, begged Lola to lend her money, manipulated my dad into sending more money that was ostensibly for something I needed, and took all the money I'd saved from doing odd jobs and from Papa's allowance and rewards.

That left Kevin.

My mom seemed to think that in order to butter up Kevin and convince him to hand over his hard-earned money, she had to pick a fight with me. I was sitting in my room reading a book after school one day when she came home. "Zachary!" she yelled. "Get your bitch ass down here, fucking pussy." As usual, I had no idea what I could have done to make her so angry. I hadn't even seen her since the day before.

"Now, who the fuck do you think you are?" she asked once I got downstairs. "You have a real nigga sitting in front of you right now," she said, gesturing at Kevin. "A strong black man." Apparently I'd disrespected him by not giving him a proper greeting when I'd gotten home from school. "If you don't show him the respect he deserves, he will put you in the fucking ground," she told me. "He will put you in the dirt."

I looked over at Kevin, who was sitting on the couch, looking proud of himself. She continued berating me until Kevin was satisfied. Then she pulled me aside and spoke to me quietly with a serious look in her eyes. "Zachary," she said, this time in a softer tone, "I have to do some things I'm not proud of, and I don't want you to see me grovel and beg, so you better get your punk ass back upstairs."

This scene played itself out time and time again. The details were always a bit different, but the pattern was the same — her making me feel small and vulnerable in order to make Kevin feel big and important. She changed up her rants frequently to keep me guessing, so that nothing she said became normalized and so that I couldn't build up an internal defense against any one argument. I always knew what road she'd go down, but I had no idea where the booby traps were laid.

I'd go back to my room and try to read or play video games to take my mind off the pain I felt, but this often wasn't easy. I think back on these episodes now, and a part of me wishes I had been able to muster the strength to respond to her anger with love and love only, to say to her warmly, "Mom, I just want you to know that I love you, that I'm sorry for upsetting you, that I'd never do anything to hurt you. I do love you, Mom, and I always will, no matter what." But her outbursts of anger temporarily diminished, and sometimes extinguished, my capacity for compassion. Being yelled at by my mom was a transformative experience; it often shook me to the core and left me devastated. Alone in my room, sometimes I cried or socked a pillow, but most of the time I asked myself why she had to attack me to make Kevin happy.

This tactic always worked to get her what she wanted, though. Kevin handed over every penny and on occasion even called several of his relatives to ask them for money. Then she'd go back to the casino until the money ran out and she would have to start all over again.

Soon after, I was at Lola's house for a visit. "Remember a long time ago when I told you some stuff about my mom?" I asked her. She seemed to be in a receptive mood, which wasn't always the case, so I continued. "I need to tell you some more stuff." I told her about the rants, the gambling, the threats, and the fact that even though she had stopped hitting me, she still hit Kevin sometimes.

Lola looked shocked. Just like the therapists and the audiences at those conventions, she had thought my mom was doing better. "Ooh-wee," she said, letting out a breath. "Your mom is crazy."

"Sometimes," I told her, "I just wish she wouldn't even come home from the casino."

Lola grew serious. "Zachary," she told me, "I will not let you go."

I had no idea what she was planning to do. When she brought me home, Lola confronted my mom about everything I'd told her. "I will not let him go," she repeated.

My mom grew enraged, but Lola refused to leave me alone with her. We had a dog at the time, a big German shepherd named Duchess. Lola was terrified of dogs, and of course my mom knew this. "Get her, Duchess, get her!" my mom commanded, trying to sic Duchess on my grandmother. I grabbed her by the collar and tried to distract Duchess by playing with her. My mom and Lola continued shouting at each other in the background.

Finally, my mom turned to me. "You will come with me," she said in such a serious tone that I was afraid to disobey. I looked at Lola, who was visibly shaken. My mom took my arm and led me outside and into her car. She took off. In the rearview mirror, I could see Lola get in her car and follow us. I didn't know where we were going. My mom did not say a word as she sped around corners and down roads with Lola in pursuit. She drove erratically around town for at least twenty minutes, constantly looking back to see if Lola was still behind us.

Finally, we came to a traffic light. With

Lola stopped behind us, my mom put the car in reverse. It was as if she were trying to back directly into Lola's car. She was so close that I could see Lola fumbling with the gearshift, trying to get out of the way. Just then the light turned green, and my mom sped off. I looked behind us again, and Lola's car was nowhere to be found.

My mom continued driving for several minutes, a bit calmer now. We ended up in front of a building I recognized. It was her therapist's office. She got out, sat down on the front steps, and took out a cigarette. Unsure of what to do, I sat down beside her. For the next twenty minutes or so, we sat in absolute silence as my mother smoked cigarette after cigarette, staring me right in the eye, her face brimming with a subdued rage.

I was terrified. No matter how much her rants may have broken me down, they never crept up on me. When I sensed she was getting angry, I could always try to say something nice and affectionate to soften her mood or build up my armor to deflect whatever she was going to say. But this was frightening, because I had no idea what she was going to do next. She was clearly furious, but it was a calm and controlled anger, delicately restrained, and that was far scarier to me than utter rage.

After what felt like a lifetime, she spoke in a perfectly calm voice. "Don't worry, Zachary," she told me, tapping on the end of her cigarette. "We're going to get you some help."

When my mother was twelve years old, she heard her father call out from his bedroom. She rushed into the room and found him on his bed, with his eyes rolling back in his head. She called 911, but it was too late. He died of a brain aneurysm.

I've come to realize that this was the precipitating event that triggered my mom's mental illness. She became extremely depressed after her father's death, but when Lola took her to see a psychologist, he said she was simply in mourning. That wasn't right. My mom remained in a state of extreme distress, which manifested itself in many different ways over the years.

Before her father died, according to my mom, she had had an idyllic childhood. Her family moved from Texas to Detroit when she was three years old. Lola and my grandfather, Bernard, were teachers, both highly educated and intelligent. My grandfather was on the school board, and they lived in a stately home in one of Detroit's nicest neighborhoods. My grandparents gave my mom as many opportunities as they could — ballet classes, Jack and Jill of America, and even debutante balls. But my mom was always mischievous. Even at a young age, she would play hooky, spend time in class daydreaming and drawing pictures instead of paying attention, or leave school during recess to go get ice cream.

My mom idolized her dad. She always held him up as the absolute epitome of what it meant to be a real man. "He was the realest nigga out there," is the way she said it to me. She was obsessed with the idea of masculinity and what it meant to be a "real nigga." "He looked at people a certain way, and they knew not to mess with him." He was strong, confident, and fearless — a black man's black man who carried a handgun, always wore a suit, and held an academic leadership position in the 1980s. I wish I'd had a chance to meet him.

But over time, as I listened closely to my mother's romanticized stories about her dad, it became clear to me that he wasn't as perfect as she claimed. For one thing, he had a violent temper. He didn't terrorize my mom for no reason, but whenever she broke a rule or acted out, which was often, he'd pick up a belt and chase her around the house. "He tore me up," she told me. Then he would calm down and apologize later.

She rarely mentioned those moments. When she talked about her dad, she almost always focused on the good things — the times he took her to get ice cream or to see a movie. I realized that a lot of the things we did on our fun-filled adventures were the same things she had enjoyed doing with her dad growing up. She always felt closer to him than she did to Lola and referred to him as her best friend and confidant.

After he died, my mom's life started to spiral out of control. She refused to listen to my grandmother, ran away from home a few times, and had trouble focusing in school. In high school, she was diagnosed with attention deficit disorder. Despite all this, my mom was very smart and always did well in school. She graduated from the University of Maryland and got a paralegal certification from the American University of Paris.

It was there that her mental illness began to take another turn. She was severely depressed and spent almost all her time alone in her room, staring at the ceiling. Shortly after coming home, she was out jogging when my dad pulled up alongside her in his car. My mom gave him her number, and he called her thirty minutes later.

My dad told me that they had a lot of fun together in the beginning. He described my mother as playful, sensitive, and emotional, but he never had any inkling that something was wrong. Interestingly, though, when I talked to him about my mom's childhood, I got the impression that he didn't believe it was as great as my mom made it out to be. I've heard the same thing in veiled words from various aunts, uncles, and cousins.

After hearing this, whenever I listened to my mom take great pains to make her father and her entire childhood seem nothing less than perfect, I started to believe that she had in fact gone through some things that she'd never shared with anyone. The truth is, her words about her dad echoed the way I spoke about her — overcompensating so that no one would think for a minute that anything was wrong.

After the day of the car chase with Lola, my mom brought me to several different therapists and told them that I may have been suffering from "episodes." Alone in the room with these mental health professionals, I wanted to tell them the truth, but I was too afraid. So I lied. I said how perfect and wonderful everything was at school and at home. They had no reason not to believe me, and they all reported back to my mom that I seemed fine; that I was driven, focused, and intelligent.

Some of these therapists were so impressed that they began inviting me to speak with my mom at mental health conferences. In front of hundreds of people, I delivered my own speeches about how proud I was of my mom for overcoming so many obstacles. I said that she was my number one fan and my best friend.

For hours at a time, often late into the night, my mom coached me on how to deliver those speeches. She taught me how to stand, how to make eye contact with individual audience members, and how to vary my facial expressions and body language throughout a speech. She gave these expressions labels — poise, passion, and instruction — and then she'd cue me as I recited a speech. "Show me poise," she commanded, and then, "now passion."

I was usually exhausted during these practices after a long day at school, but if I missed a cue, I'd get in trouble. "I said, show me poise, Zachary. Do you know how much I do for you, you ungrateful bitch-ass nigga?" She sat up and tapped her cigarette on the side of the ashtray. Tap, tap, tap.

"Show me poise, or I'll have Kevin come in here and show you what strength looks like."

I fixed my posture, tilted my head slightly, and cupped my palms, gesturing with them in a controlled manner as I spoke, my voice gliding over the words with easy modulation, just as Bill Clinton had done in the video she'd showed me earlier. She looked pleased. "Now start over from the beginning."

This training paid off when I started at Grosse Pointe Academy that same year. My mom prepared me in other ways, too. On our way to school on my first day, my mom told me, "Make sure you tell them that your grandmother was an educator and that your grandparents are well traveled. Make sure they know you can swim." My mom was trying to help me learn my way in the new world I was entering — a world of wealth and privilege.

The atmosphere at GPA was completely different from that at my public school. There were other kids who loved learning and reading as much as I did, and the teachers were involved and engaged. My teacher, Mr. Lapadot, made learning fun by integrating academic decathlon games into the classroom and creating an economy in the classroom by rewarding us with tickets for doing extra assignments. We could save up our tickets and then use them to buy snacks or toys at auctions he held at the end of every month.

This propelled me forward and brought out my competitive instincts. I went from being a good student to going above and beyond. At one point, I had more than twice as many tickets as anyone else in the classroom. But the best part of being at GPA was how open the teachers were to listening to my ideas and answering my questions. Here my questions weren't a burden; they were welcomed, even encouraged. Nothing was sacrosanct. This expanded my mind more than anything else I'd experienced, and even then I thought how unfair it was that my former classmates at the public school I'd attended didn't have access to such an open and stimulating learning environment.

It didn't take me long to prove myself there, but when I first started at GPA, a few of the teachers and parents I met took one look at me and asked if I played basketball. It seemed they assumed that my main contribution to the school would be in athletics. They surmised other things, too. Even when I was at the center of everything, I constantly felt as if I was on the outside looking in. In my first year there, I had plenty of friends, but I wasn't really one of them. I didn't come from their neighborhood. I wasn't a part of their community. And many of their comments and jokes, impersonations of stereotypes about black people, and presumptions that my family loved fried chicken and Kool-Aid reminded me of this.

There was one other black boy in my entire grade, Derrick, and all the other kids loved him because he was the class clown. When they asked him to impersonate cartoon characters, comedians, or a stereotypical thug, he played along. I knew he was doing it just to fit in, not because he really wanted to, and I felt for him, but I hated to see him doing all that to get the other kids' attention.

This was not my style. Instead of playing to stereotypes, I was determined to use the same resource that helped me escape my world at home to fit into this new world — my mind. I wanted to prove their assumptions wrong by showing them through my behavior and academic performance that I was more than they expected.

But when I saw these new friends outside of school, I felt like even more of an outsider. They didn't just live in homes that were larger than mine. Many of them lived in lavish mansions with guesthouses and pool houses twice the size of my house, and full-length tennis and basketball courts in the backyard. When I looked through the last names in the student directory for the first time, I realized whom I was going to school with: students whose families had founded entire retail and automotive industries and owned major furniture companies, restaurant chains, and popular sports franchises like the Red Wings and the Tigers.

To my new friends, all this was normal. To me, eating dinner inside of palatial mansions with eight bedrooms and maid service was like being in a fantasyland. I knew that families of great wealth and privilege lived in Grosse Pointe Farms, but I never knew quite what their life was like until I experienced it myself.

When I went over to friends' houses, the first thing I noticed was the convenience of it all. These kids could have whatever they wanted whenever they wanted it. And when they didn't get it, they'd throw a fit, arguing with their parents and making demands. They even called their parents by their first names. This was a complete shock to me. I never would have dared to speak to my mom that way; plus I couldn't imagine what these kids had to complain about. Their lives seemed so stable and comfortable. They knew what to expect from day to day. Everything was just so easy.

As much as my mom tried to prepare me for this, she didn't like me spending too much time at friends' houses. Sometimes she would make difficult demands — that I could go to their house but I was not allowed to eat their food or use their bathroom. This confounded me. If she didn't want me to experience these things, why did she spend so much time coaching me on manners, etiquette, and how to speak to these people in a way that was eloquent and graceful?

The one thing she stressed more than anything else was the importance of never conveying anger. "You are a black man, Zachary," she told me from a very young age. "You can be assertive, but you have to be composed and tread delicately, or you'll become associated with things that will never help you."

In her calmer moments, she explained the fear associated with black masculinity and self-assertion, that centuries of slavery and oppression had restrained the ways black men had been able to embody a sense of agency. Slave masters sought to destroy a black man's manhood by beating and degrading him, calling him "nigger," and taking away everything that mattered to him. In great detail, she explained how during slavery there was nothing black men could take pride in. Their lives were miserable and it may have made their blood boil, but they couldn't assert themselves physically or verbally. They had to be totally submissive.

This was why, she told me, black people walked around feeling acted upon. It was their legacy that things would just happen to them and there was nothing they could do about it. She told me to never ask, "What's going to happen?" or "What are you going to do?" This was too passive. She saw the people I was interacting with in this new world as the descendants of slave owners, and in some cases they were. It was important to her that when I was with them I not feel weak or intimidated. I didn't have the money or resources they had, but I could be socially dominant. So she taught me to be witty, crisp, and sleek, with no hard edges and just the right amount of swagger.

Yet it was just as important to her that I could be a "real nigga" and fit in with the guys in our neighborhood. She brought me over to her friend Yeti's apartment and told

77

him, "Zachary's soft. He's a pussy."

Yeti was intimidating and tough, and he told me, "You can't let those niggas out there punk you, man." I studied Yeti — the way he slouched, the way he leaned, the way he walked and talked and the slang he used. Later my mom made me practice. Then she dropped me off at a basketball court in a rough area close to where we lived. There, on the basketball court, everything my mom had taught me about black masculinity was manifest.

I already knew how important basketball was to most guys in my neighborhood. But now I realized why. These kids didn't go to a school like GPA where curiosity was encouraged. They didn't have music lessons and swimming lessons, but they did have basketball. Basketball was free and the court was their turf, the one place where they could fully express themselves and feel a certain amount of dignity and self-respect. So they had to go hard, and they did.

I was quiet at first. I tried to use some of what I'd learned from Yeti and act a little tough so that I'd blend in but not too tough that I'd stand out and make myself a target. I knew some of the other boys from around the neighborhood. They always saw me as a bit of an outsider. I wasn't one of them. I didn't talk or dress like them, and I was more interested in reading than in hanging out with them. So they treated me with a mix of skepticism and mild hostility.

I didn't exactly blame them. Those kids were tough. For years, they'd been fighting to survive. During the basketball games, the kids my age were getting elbowed and knocked down by older boys, but they kept on getting up. They had no choice.

These were my first experiences with code switching — going back and forth between two distinct worlds. I got better and better at it, but I always felt that I was playing a role, presenting some kind of spin-off of who I actually was.

Papa, more than anyone, helped me navigate this. He'd often take me out to nice restaurants and teach me such things as which fork to use for which course. Papa had more life experiences than anyone I knew, so I asked him question after question about all sorts of things I had heard and observed at school. I remember asking him, "What's it like in Aspen?" and "What is a stock?"

Papa had been to Aspen, so he told me about it, and then he patiently explained the stock market and how money grows over time. He told me that some of these families weren't wealthy just because they had good jobs and earned a lot of money. These families had old money that had accrued over centuries; some of them had amassed wealth from slavery. The picture Papa painted was that privilege was both self-sustaining and complicated.

"Wealth makes it easier for them to feel like they don't have to be conscientious," he told me. "They have the means and the resources to get their own way. The pressures are different for you." He told me that I had to be conscientious and articulate, and then explained to me why people rarely describe a white person as articulate. He was right. I've never heard a white peer be referred to as articulate, but I've been described that way to my face a hundred times.

Papa did a good job of explaining to me subtle contours of the inner feelings of white people, the preconceptions they're often not even aware of that lie beneath the surface. It was a contrast to the highly reactive way my mom handled these conversations. As soon as I'd started at Grosse Pointe, when I got home from school I had to give my mom an extremely detailed account of everything I had done throughout the day. If I left anything out, even something

80

insignificant, she'd blow up at me. If my reports included a racially charged joke or comment, she grew furious, often blowing it out of proportion.

When a classmate imitated the way a black NBA player walked, and the art teacher, who was also my basketball coach, laughed, my mom called my dad and told him that he had to call the teacher and tell him off. After this incident, my mom told me to "man up" and whenever I saw the principal to tell him that I was displeased with how I was being treated at GPA. As with everything I had ever been told to do by my mother, these orders were nonnegotiable. Over similar incidents, she later confronted the principal and had one of the leading lawyers in Detroit write a letter to the headmaster, stating that the school was acting in a discriminatory fashion.

To me, all these incidents, while obnoxious sometimes, seemed more naive than malicious. Besides me and Derrick, most of the black people my classmates had been exposed to were either serving them food or on TV. So they often assumed that I was the exception that proved the rule. When I visited their homes, I saw exactly where these attitudes came from. I was shocked to see how frequently race came up at their dinner tables, whether it was to talk about how the test scores at colleges were going to go up if more Asian students enrolled, or the fact that Mexicans can never be trusted.

One time, I was at a friend's house when a story came on the news about a black criminal who had killed two white people. It was an extreme and violent story — completely outside of my reality. But my friend's father turned to me and said, "Zach, I'm so glad that you have a good head on your shoulders and understand appropriate decorum." I didn't understand. Was he comparing me to this murderer? Then he added, "A friend of mine is thinking of running for the school board; he should use you in his campaign."

I didn't have the words for it then, but I sensed that they were exceptionalizing me. They held on to the idea that black people were not meant to achieve. My achievements at GPA were so rare, such a contrast to the representations of black people they saw in the media. But the idea that my success should be lauded as an example for others to follow made me feel uncomfortable. To suggest that they were racist would be unfair, and I don't believe many of them were, but they didn't seem to understand that plenty of black kids would have been high achieving if they had had the same types of opportunities I'd found.

A few days later, I was playing outside in my neighborhood when one of the kids I knew from the basketball court came up to me. "What up, nigga?" he asked bitterly, with a hostile look on his face.

"Call me Zach, man," I said, trying not to let him punk me.

"Nigga, I'll call you whatever I want," he said angrily, and then he came up and pushed me. We threw a few punches, and then he ran home and told his mom. Within minutes, his mother was in front of our house, cursing out my mom, who came outside and met her on the street.

"Fuck you, bitch! You better tell your boy not to put his hands on my son," the other mother said threateningly.

"No, fuck you, bitch, your son should have never started it," my mom responded.

As they continued screaming at each other, I looked around at the small crowd that was gathering and thought about my school friends' parents. It was so clear to me what they would have thought if they saw this on the news. I could practically hear them saying, "It's such a shame that these people don't know any better."

As I was learning to code-switch to fit into

different environments, I began to understand how I could alter my behavior to appease my mom. I was always trying to find a way to quell her rage and increase the frequency of her happy-go-lucky days, so I started testing how my behavior affected her. What would happen if I gave her good news? What about if I complimented her?

The one thing that consistently worked to soften up my mom was for me to give her a warm hug and say that I loved her and wanted to spend more time with her. Then she was affectionate and more receptive to my questions. I was forcing myself to show her compassion in order to gain a small understanding for how she saw the world. Although it would have been very tough at times, now that I'm older, I wish I would have made that effort more often. Meanwhile, I began to research her disease to better understand the neurological components and the symptoms. I think "schizophrenia" was the first thing I typed into Google when I got my first computer. Then, whenever she lashed out at me, I tried to empathize by reminding myself of what was going on in her brain.

Mostly, I learned that her behavior was unpredictable. Yet there were times when her symptoms were well under control. GPA held a knowledge fair, where parents would come in and speak about different subjects. My mom volunteered to talk about health and nutrition because she wanted to disabuse my peers and their families of the notion that I came from a black family that ate only fast food and soul food. I was nervous beforehand, wondering if she would make a scene, but on the day of the event she was all smiles. She knew exactly how to talk to my friends and keep them engaged while showing a mother's loving favoritism for me. Watching my friends responding so well to her, I felt proud that she was my mom. Throughout my time at GPA, there were several moments like this.

But there was one thing that I knew would always throw her into a rage, and that was when I asserted my desire to see my dad. I really missed my dad during these years. I was allowed to contact him by phone or e-mail only once every two weeks, and when he came up for a visit, my mom kept a tight rein on me. I could barely enjoy my time with him because I had to call her to check in so frequently.

One time, my dad drove all the way to Detroit to visit me and attend Dads' Day at GPA, another annual event at the school. I was beyond excited to see my dad; it had been almost six months since his last visit. On our way to school, he glimpsed the extraordinary wealth and grandeur that I'd described in our phone conversations. Looking out the window as he drove, he saw gated communities populated with sprawling estates, the immaculate tracery of their manicured landscapes covered by a thin blanket of snow.

As we pulled into the main driveway of GPA's campus, my dad was in awe of the campus's French Gothic and Colonial architecture. "I've never seen an elementary school that looked like this," he told me. But what stood out the most wasn't the school's range of ornate facades; it was the waterfront. The school's main building was rectangular, made of red brick and stone blocks, and rested prominently atop a verdant slope, just yards away from the rippling currents of the Detroit River.

Throughout the day, my dad got to meet my friends and their fathers. He was from a very different background than most of the other dads and didn't share the same wealth and status, but he didn't seem intimidated or bothered by that at all. He was confident and gracious and happy to be there with me. Mostly, he was pleased to see firsthand what an excellent education I was receiving.

To give our dads a sense of what class was like on a daily basis, Mr. Lapadot had us run through a competitive series of academic games. We covered everything from logic puzzles and long-division problems at the blackboard to spelling, grammar, and historical and geographical trivia. I loved Mr. Lapadot's class, and I was glad that my dad got a chance to see me excel in the classroom.

My dad told me afterward that he was most surprised by how many capitals I'd memorized. By that point in the school year, I'd memorized the capitals and leaders of almost every country in Europe and Asia, and I could list the names of every United States president in order and note a fun fact about most of them. I explained to my dad that in Mr. Lapadot's class, we were given maps of continents to study and then tested on our knowledge of geography, and because I had a good memory, I aced every map test. I told him that I wanted to learn more about the economies and histories of these different countries next.

As he listened to me go on and on about this, I could tell how proud he was that I was doing so well at GPA, especially considering how different my circumstances were from those of my classmates. When I finally stopped talking about my interest in geography, he shook his head ruefully. "It has not been easy making those payments," he told me. "But it's worth it, Main Man. I'm gonna do everything I can to keep you here."

My mom had other ideas. Over time, her overreactions to perceived slights began to escalate. The winter I was in sixth grade, a few friends and I got into a snowball fight during recess. When I reported this to my mom after school, she asked me, "Did you win?"

I hesitated, knowing that if I admitted to not winning the snowball fight, she'd call me a punk. "Yeah, I won," I said.

"No, you didn't," she told me sternly. "I was watching you from my car, and I saw the whole thing. Now, what did that white boy say when he hit you with the snowball?"

My mom did this sometimes, just showed up and spied on me without my knowing. It was one of the main reasons I usually tried to do what she said, even when I thought she wasn't around. "He said, 'I got you,' " I told her.

"Tell me what he said, Zachary," she said angrily.

I sighed. "He said, 'I own you,' " I said, "but it wasn't like that."

She cut me off before I had a chance to finish. "He said he owned you?!" She was livid. She went to the administration, and over the next few days, the boys involved in the snowball fight had to see the dean and sit through meetings with the principal. I felt bad that they were getting into trouble when I knew they hadn't really meant any harm, but my mom made it clear that I was to play along and make sure everyone knew I was suffering in this hostile environment. Of course, these kids and some of my other friends started holding things like this against me.

I was still doing well in school academically, but I began to struggle to fit in. I had great grades, and I excelled in particular at forensics, or public speaking. My experience speaking at mental health conventions and being trained by my mom was paying off. I consistently got perfect scores on my speeches and won eight first-place awards in the Eastern Catholic Forensics League's declamation category. I also performed extremely well in the school-wide spelling bee, competing, in the end, against two eighth-graders. Although I finished in third place, the three of us went back and forth for a record-breaking eighty-eight rounds, so long that the administration had to come up with a new spelling list. The previous year, the school spelling bee had consisted of only twenty-two rounds. The next day, a story about the event made its way into the local newspaper.

But school was no longer a purely positive place where I could focus exclusively on doing my best. I was losing friends and was constantly worried that my mom would show up and create some sort of conflict. It seemed that whenever I was doing well or was proud of something, she found a way to ruin it — even forensics. When a white classmate's mother edited one of my speeches, changing the word *blacker* to *bleaker,* my mom confronted the woman face-to-face and tried to intimidate her.

With fewer friends than I'd ever had before, I started to spend more time after class talking to teachers. I found that if I tried to be helpful to them, these teachers appreciated me. I suppose I was looking for positive attention and validation from an adult, something I wasn't getting at home. There was one teacher in particular who was more than happy for me to spend time after school helping her. I spent hours in her classroom, helping her with various menial tasks. Occasionally, I even helped her with personal tasks that had nothing to do with school. She loved me for it, and I liked how it felt to be valued for having done something positive.

That teacher ran something called Blue Crew, a student group that advertised school paraphernalia, ran concession stands, and operated the scoreboards at athletic events. None of the other kids wanted to join Blue Crew that year because it had become a bit tedious and demanding, so I did all the work that was normally shared by up to ten people. I did everything, from setting up the stands and keeping score to selling the concessions and figuring out various logistical details. At the end of the season, the school gave me a sweater from the school store and a certificate as a reward for my hard work, and my mom was upset because she thought I deserved a trophy.

It was always something. In seventh grade, I had done better than another boy on a vocabulary test and we had a little argument about it. We tossed a few insults back and forth, and then he said, "At least I don't have nappy hair." Then he pushed me. I pushed him back, and then he swung at me. I ducked.

In the next millisecond it felt as if a million thoughts were swimming through my mind at once. My first and most salient thought was that if I shied away from a fight with this kid, my mom would somehow find out and berate me for being a bitch, a punk. She would make me feel worthless, like an utter failure. At the same time, I was thinking how badly I didn't want to hit this boy. His family probably already thought that black people fought all the time, and if I hit back, I would just be playing into that stereotype.

I swung back. We each threw a couple of punches, and I ended up in the principal's office. I didn't really understand why the other kid wasn't in trouble, too, especially since he had swung at me first. The principal spoke to me sternly about fighting, but since this was my first time doing anything wrong, there was no punishment.

My mom was much harder on me than the principal had been. She was mad that I hadn't fought back harder and yelled at me for hours, threatening to send me out to the worst part of town in the middle of the night to toughen me up. She told me that her father would have been disappointed in me, that he would have beaten my ass because I'd been taught better than that, and that I'd better man up or get the hell out of her house. By this point, I was resilient. But she had an endless reservoir of ways to break me down and emasculate me. I knew she was sick and wrong. I also knew she was proud of my accomplishments, but sometimes when I lay in bed at night I wondered what, if anything, would make her proud of the man I was developing into.

When she was done with me, my mom got a lawyer to threaten to sue the school for fostering racism. She thought that she was protecting me from people who treated me badly, and though she had blown much out of proportion and only made things worse, I can understand, and even appreciate, her refusal to let me endure what she saw as injustice.

In the end, her battle with GPA's administration was a fiasco. I was embarrassed and anxious and ultimately felt a small amount of relief when my mom started talking about pulling me out of GPA and sending me to another school. I vowed to myself that when I got to a new school, I'd never tell her the truth about what was going on so that she wouldn't have anything to hold against me.

And that's exactly what I did.

CHAPTER 3
ONE CALL

I left GPA in the middle of seventh grade and transferred to the Roeper School. Roeper was in Birmingham, Michigan, an affluent suburb about forty-five minutes from GPA. The culture at Roeper was completely different from that at GPA or at any other school I'd been to. Everyone there was smart, but the school focused on self-development and depth of learning rather than on broad academic achievement. Students were free to pour themselves into whatever they were passionate about, whether that was piano, history, or collecting rare insects. There were no spelling bees or academic awards. The emphasis was on creativity and radical individualism.

I loved it, but it was definitely a shock to my system. I had gotten used to the uniformed, prep-school vibe at GPA, and Roeper was liberal and profoundly tolerant. There was no cafeteria or designated lunch period. Students had one or two hours of free time a day, during which they could paint, draw, study, eat lunch, or even take a nap in the principal's office. We called all the teachers and the administrative staff by their first names.

Even the assignments were more flexible than the ones I was used to. Instead of having to write an essay about a specific topic, we could write about whatever interested us most about a book we'd read. At that point, a big part of my identity was wrapped up in academic achievement, but that wasn't valued at Roeper the way I'd expected it to be. Sure, the teachers wanted us to do well, but grades were less important than personal expression. So I struggled at first to reconcile my ambition and the pressure I had put on myself to perform academically with this new set of values.

When starting at Roeper, my main priority, though, was for things to go smoothly for once. I had switched schools so many times that I never felt that I could really get comfortable anywhere, and part of me blamed myself for having to leave GPA. If only I had lied to my mom better or assuaged her concern, I thought, or been a real man, maybe I could have stayed. It was stressful and exhausting to keep starting

95

over, and I was determined to not have to go through that again.

Luckily, there was such a positive community vibe at Roeper that I didn't have to lie to my mom to avoid telling her anything negative during my daily after-school reports, which continued. There just wasn't anything troubling to share. Unlike at my previous schools, the boundaries between the black and the white students weren't so sharp. My classmates all seemed more aware and more thoughtful. I could tell that they saw me differently than my friends had at GPA. They didn't look at me as the one exceptional black kid and make assumptions about me, and I in turn found myself questioning a lot of my own assumptions.

I met kids at Roeper who were unlike anyone I'd been exposed to before — privileged white kids who were doing more to actively fight racism than I was, and black kids from the inner city who were deeply engaged in a variety of passions and interests. I realized I couldn't assume that just because some people were white and well-off, they had a certain attitude about race. At the same time, people's circumstances didn't necessarily dictate how they engaged with the world around them.

I remember trying to describe some of

these kids to my dad. "There's this big black kid with an Afro," I told him. "Dude is the most soft-spoken guy, and all he talks about is Steven Tyler and Lynyrd Skynyrd." My dad and I shared a laugh over this, but I actually learned a good bit from that kid. He and many of the other students at Roeper made me realize that diversity existed in a multiplicity of ways and a variety of forms. There was diversity of thought and personality, and as I engaged with a wider spectrum of people and ideas than ever before, I saw that this variety added value.

This also complemented my understanding of affirmative action. When I was growing up, my mom had a way of explaining complicated issues in ways that I could understand. She taught me from a young age that one of the key tensions in American life was between achievement and equality. Democrats, she said, usually fought for the little guy, whereas Republicans tended to value tradition and favor ideas and policies that benefited the affluent.

Race-based affirmative action, she explained, was generally supported by Democrats and not Republicans because Democrats thought of affirmative action as a strategy that sought to make up, however inadequately, for centuries of racial oppression and the lingering effects that have persisted. That made sense to me. But my mom also wanted me to understand the significant moral and social costs of affirmative action and that there were legitimate reasons for people to oppose it.

By giving special favoritism to black students, affirmative action often disadvantaged other groups, such as hardworking white and Asian students. Lower standards for admission could also have the effect of diminishing incentives for black students to work as hard as they could, diluting the American ideal of meritocracy, she explained. On top of that, my mom pointed out that giving people access and opportunity doesn't always mean they have the tools and resources necessary to make the most of them.

My experience at Roeper prompted me to think about affirmative action in new ways. While I still strongly supported sensible race-based affirmative action as a form of compensatory justice and a means of ensuring diversity, I began to support class- and gender-based affirmative action, as well.

In addition to reading the work of various scholars who had written about the issue, thinking about my own experience and the sharp disparities in the quality of education between certain public and private schools deepened my appreciation of the affirmative-action ethos. I saw the value of having diverse voices and opinions among those in positions of cultural authority and political power. In this sense, I realized, affirmative action was about giving people who would not otherwise have them the access and opportunity that could enhance their chances of achieving and contributing meaningfully to society.

As I had at GPA, I worked tirelessly at Roeper to fill my days with positive experiences and productivity to compensate for how unhappy I often was at home. But these experiences weren't strictly academic. I still spent a lot of time reading and doing homework, but I spent more time than ever on the basketball court. Basketball became an outlet, a way to relieve stress and express the competitive instincts that weren't encouraged in the classrooms. On most days, I got to school more than an hour early and played basketball, I played during my free period at school, and I often played after school or in my neighborhood on the weekends.

I was thirteen and also began having new and exciting social experiences. At Roeper,

I felt free to be myself, and I was learning who that was through friendships, in-depth conversations, and, before long, dating. At Roeper, everyone was open about everything. For the first time, girls were interested in me, and instead of flirting or sending mixed messages, they came right up and said, "I like you; let's go out." Soon, I had my first girlfriend, my first kiss, even my first time breaking a rule when we snuck off campus to go eat at Qdoba or to get ice cream at Sanders.

The freedom I enjoyed while at school was a complete contrast to my experiences at home. My mom couldn't keep me from growing up, but she did everything she could to keep me under her control. She read my texts and e-mails, listened in on my phone calls, and always made me leave the door to my room open so that she could see and hear exactly what I was doing. She even tried to exercise control over my burgeoning sexuality, offering me porn, asking me in graphic detail about how my body was changing, and forcing me to listen to Lil' Kim songs so that she could explain the lyrics to me.

My mom couldn't take me to bars or clubs — I was only thirteen — so she'd drive me to the entrance of one late at night, and we'd sit in the car and watch the people coming out. She taught me to pick up on the subtlest clues, the secret messages being passed between men and women that I was too young to fully understand. "Look at his facial expression," she'd tell me as we watched a man talking to a woman. "It's forced. That makes him look insecure." She taught me that confidence — or the lack of it — is revealed in everything you do: how you hold your hands, how you walk, the angle of your chin. To her, this all went back to sexual prowess. But as I learned to internalize these cues, I began to use them to connect more authentically with people.

Half of the time, it seemed that she wanted to empower me so that I knew how to get what I wanted in the world, while the rest of the time she brutally cut me down. After my mom found out about my girlfriend by reading my text messages, she punished me by asking me to go to the grocery store with her and then locking me out of the car. It was winter, and I stood outside in the freezing cold as she drove away. I didn't have a key to the condo, so I couldn't get back inside. Ten minutes later, I got a text from her: "Zachary, you better get your bitch ass in this car."

I ran down the street to catch up to her

and found her pulled over to the side of the road, calmly smoking a cigarette. I got in, and we drove in silence. My fingers were still numb from the cold, and I was upset, but my silence infuriated her. She pulled over right on the side of the highway and just glared at me with that look on her face.

"No woman should ever take my place, do you understand me, boy?"

"Yes, I understand," I replied.

"Don't make me leave you out here stranded on the freeway. I gave birth to your black ass. I raised you; I clothed you; I fed you. I will not come second to whoever this bitch is. Have I made myself clear, Zachary?"

"Yes," I replied.

"So," she said, taking a drag of her cigarette, "tell me about the bitch."

For the next half hour, we sat in the car as she grilled me about my girlfriend in explicit detail. What did her body look like? What kind of kisser was she? What did I want to do with her when we were alone? It was the last thing I wanted to discuss.

When we got back home, she said that I needed to learn how to dance like a real man, the way her father used to dance with Lola. So she brought in Kevin to dance with her. "Let a real man show you how it's done," she said. Then she put on Tupac Shakur's "Hail Mary" and made me dance around the room with her. "Mama told me never stop until I bust a nut," she sang along, and then smacked me on the ass and squeezed hard.

These moments were so uncomfortable, so surreal, that I often survived only by imagining myself looking in from the outside. What would people think if they saw this? I wondered. What would they assume about her — about me? The next day at school, I was always worried that people could tell, that they could smell it on me that I'd been through hell.

That year, we moved from our condo in the city to a house in the suburbs that was close to Roeper in a much safer, nicer neighborhood. Kevin was making more money, and he and my mom had gotten married the year before. It was the first time since I had left the public school that I was living in the same neighborhood as the kids I went to school with, and my social life continued to flourish. The house was built on an A-frame and got narrower as it went up. My room was on the top floor. When I first saw the house, I thought this meant I would have more privacy, but I was mistaken. Under no circumstances was I allowed to close that door. When I was in my room reading or studying or talking on the phone, my mom would often sit on the stairs right inside the doorway, just listening. It was frustrating, and I hated it, constantly worrying, wondering if she was spying on me or eavesdropping. At times it even made me anxious. I'd get up from my desk and walk over to the stairwell periodically just to see if she was there.

The summer after seventh grade I went to DC to spend a couple of months with my dad. He and Brenda had split up, and my dad had moved in with his mother, my grandma Pearl. Her health was declining and her longtime partner had passed away, so my dad wanted to be there to help take care of her. My grandmother's small house was in a rough part of DC and hadn't been well maintained. I slept on a small cot in the living room, and it was far less comfortable than our house in Michigan, but I loved being there with my dad.

I spent that entire summer reading, playing basketball, and, when she was around, spending time with my sister, Nicole. It was a period of huge intellectual growth for me. I had become fascinated by the Founding Fathers in school, and I wanted to know what thinkers had influenced them and our democracy. So I started reading the great philosophers. At first, I'd hoped that reading modern philosophy would help me develop my own grand philosophical idea. Soon enough, I realized I'd never have an idea half as influential as any of Plato's, yet I could use his reasoning to strengthen my own.

My father saw it differently. He wanted me to take a break and have fun, and he worried about me when he came home from work and found me sitting in the same place reading where I'd been when he left early that morning. But by then I knew that knowledge was power, and it was the only kind of power I had access to. I was determined no matter what it took to gain as much of it as I could.

When Nicole was around, though, I was happy to take a break from reading and hang out with her. She was only six years old, but she wanted to do everything I was doing. So I told her to pick any topic she was interested in and I'd teach her about it. That summer we covered everything from the three branches of government to how her toys were made. As Papa had taught me, I still stopped reading whenever I found a word I didn't know, and looked it up. I kept track of these words and used them to make vocabulary lists for Nicole. Together, we would go over these words and others she'd ask me about. We'd use them in sentences and laugh together at the funny way she pronounced words, such as *bureaucracy.*

When I went back to Michigan to start eighth grade, I was more determined than ever to achieve all that I could. It was a goal that helped me avoid internalizing the painful things my mom said to me. I was driven to succeed in spite of her. With my mom, there was never any room for error. She'd explode over the smallest things, like breaking eye contact or not standing upright as she berated me for hours.

She didn't care so much about my grades, but I carried that sense of perfectionism to school with me. If it was possible with extra credit to get above 100, then I wanted to earn the highest possible grade. When I fell short, I'd be disappointed. But it wasn't enough for me just to do well. I wanted to feel that I had earned my achievements, that I was working harder than anyone else. I couldn't extinguish the fear she instilled in me, so I learned to translate that fear into hard work and vigilance.

That drive and competitive spirit came out on the basketball court more than anywhere. At Roeper, to get onto the high school basketball team, players had to go through something called "Hell Week," an intense week of grueling physical training. I was only in eighth grade. I didn't have to go through Hell Week, but I went anyway. It was brutal, but I was proud of myself when the JV coach saw how determined I was and asked me to practice with them. I also enjoyed hearing how excited my dad was when I told him about this. It was always hard to connect with my dad emotionally. He said so little, but sports were one thing we could always talk about.

I went above and beyond academically, too, spending my free period at school talking to teachers and students about a wide array of topics and staying up late into the night reading, studying, and learning as much as I could. I'd always had a difficult relationship with sleep, and it was around this time that I started sleeping less and less. I knew sleep was important for good health, but I also thought too much sleep was a waste of time. Plus, many of the leaders and thinkers I admired often worked late into the night. As I saw it, I could accomplish more, learn more, and do more if I spent less time sleeping. While that's all true, I was often encouraged — by teachers and family — to get more sleep.

Every so often, my mom went through a good period during which she regained faith in her therapist and seemed to be taking her meds. She'd sit me down and tell me, "Mommy's going to get better, Zach." Over the next few weeks she'd go to therapy consistently, and then she'd stop. It was during one of these periods that she started to become concerned about my perfectionism, as she called it, and the little amount of sleep I was getting. She arranged for me to meet with Reanne Young, the psychological consultant at Roeper. My first meeting with Reanne was brief and pleasant. We talked about my goals and ambitions, and she told me to reach out if I ever felt like talking more.

I liked Reanne right away. She was Asian but had grown up in a black community. She was cool, and she really seemed to understand the world I came from. Of course, there was a big part of me that wanted to tell her more — about the constant invasion of privacy, the yelling late into the night, and the extreme discomfort I felt when my mom talked at length about sexual prowess, how my body was developing, and what it meant to be a real man. But I was too afraid. I didn't know if Reanne would report back to my mom — my mom had been the one to set up that meeting. And she had a way of inserting herself into situations and showing up when I didn't expect her to.

Just a few weeks later, I was warming up before a basketball game when a group of older girls came over and started talking to me. They were flirting a little, nothing major. But when I looked over to the stands, I saw my mother sitting there, glaring at me. She looked furious. If someone else had seen her, they would have thought that something horrible had happened. She stared at me with that same expression on her face throughout the entire game. I could barely focus because I was so worried about what I was going to have to face at home later.

Sure enough, that night was rough. "You pussy-ass nigga," she taunted. "You couldn't even score. Who the hell do you think you are, Zachary?" After going off on me, she started attacking the girls I'd been talking to, calling them low-class skanks and demanding to know in detail what I imagined doing with them.

Only a few days later, I was taking a shower after basketball practice. I got out, wrapped a towel around myself, and headed upstairs to my room. On the way, my mother called me. "Zachary, come here." I could tell by the tone of her voice that something bad was coming. I reluctantly entered her room, holding the towel around my waist. "Take it off," she commanded. She was lying back in her bed, smoking a cigarette. The expression on her face was a challenge. I just stood there. "I said take it off," she repeated, her face growing angry.

"Mom, what are you talking about?"

"You know exactly what I'm talking about," she told me. "Take it off." Again, I just stood there in silence, trying to bide my time until I could find a way out of there. My mother sat up straight and tightened her eye contact. "Come on, now, Zachary. Let me take a peek," she said snidely. "I am your mother. If anyone should see it, it's me."

I had never been more uncomfortable in my life. There were times when I was more afraid, but I had never been this uncomfortable. I'd seen that look on her face before, and I knew that if I didn't obey, she would make me pay. I just kept thinking that if I listened, it would be over and I could finally leave. All I could think about was getting out of that room. I took off the towel. She just stared at me from across the room, tilting her head this way and that, as if to get a good look.

"Hmm," she said, as if she were considering things. "How much bigger does it get when it's hard?" I was humiliated, but I refused to show it. "Boy, they say you're a genius," she said sarcastically, "and you can't answer a simple question?"

By that point in my life, I could withstand a lot. I rarely cried. But I didn't trust my voice, so I held a straight face and did my best to appear unfazed. "Well, I'll tell you this," she said, finally seeming satisfied. "You're on your way, but Kevin's still got you." She laughed. Actually laughed. "Yeah, he's still got you. Now, go on, get out of here."

Over the next few weeks, I did what I could to avoid speaking to my mother. At school, I continued to excel, but inside I was fed up. The question I kept asking myself was, if this was what she was doing to me now, what would be next? What would life with her be like a year from now?

I tried to ignore her when possible. My strategy was to do things around the house before she asked so that she would have no reason to speak to me. Sometimes I swept the floor and made her bed or washed and ironed the clothes and shoveled the snow. I even walked to the grocery store once and carried everything home on foot. I was exhausted, but, worse, it wasn't working. She still found things to complain about.

The following week, I passed Reanne in the hallway and something inside me snapped. "I was wondering if I could talk to you about some things," I told her.

"Sure, Zach," she said, smiling. "Why don't you come to my office this afternoon?"

Once I was in Reanne's office, I didn't know what to say. So I went back to the perfectionism that had been the topic of our first meeting, explaining that it was important to me not to upset my mom. "Sometimes I do feel like I have to be perfect," I told her. "There's no room for imperfection with my mom, or else she gets really upset."

"I've seen the way you walk down the hall," Reanne told me. "I've seen the way you handle yourself. You don't have to worry about what your mom thinks." I always left her office feeling better than I had when I'd walked in. But it took a few more meetings before I felt comfortable telling her about how my mom berated me, watched me, and made me feel like I'd never be a real man. And several more meetings after that, I finally told her about what had happened after I'd gotten out of the shower. That's when she looked at me and said, "We need to talk about the fact that you're being abused."

I felt my eyes go wide. That word was strong and overwhelming, and it made everything so real. "I don't know if that's true," I said. "My mom's just volatile." Suddenly, the implications of everything I'd told Reanne hit me. If she told anyone, I had no idea what my mom would do. I was shaking when I looked up at Reanne and said, "Please don't tell my mom. I cannot have her find out that I told you this." Right away, she assured me that she wouldn't.

But once the truth was out, it felt as if it had a momentum all its own. I continued to meet with Reanne once every week or so, and talking to her was helpful. She told me that she had spoken to the headmaster, Randall Dunn, about what was going on with me at home, and that he had also promised not to say anything to my mom. Randall asked to meet with me and was incredibly kind and supportive. I thought that if I had this small network of support at school, then maybe I could make it. They kept their promise not to tell anyone, yet they constantly reminded me that they were there to help if anything bad happened. I remember Randall telling me, "It only takes one call, Zach."

Their support bolstered me, and it seemed that the more people I had in my corner at school, the easier it would be to survive at home. I had always felt a connection to my English teacher, Lisa Bagchi. I often sat with her during my free period and discussed the books we were reading in class. We had just finished reading *Oliver Twist,* and Lisa shared some details of her life with me that made me think she might understand what I'd been through. "Most people don't know this," I told her, "but parts of my childhood were rough." I told Lisa a few details. Not everything. But I told her about how my mom used to beat me when I was little and that she tried to offer me porn. Lisa was horrified.

Until I told the truth to Lisa and Reanne, I don't think I let myself fully absorb how bad all of this really was. I knew my mom was sick and that her behavior was deeply wrong, and I felt like I hated her at times for some of the things she said and did to me. But seeing the faces of these two grown women absolutely crumble as they listened to me talk about what I'd been through — women who were closer to my mom's age than my own and who had surely experienced their own hardships — I finally registered how others perceived my mom's actions.

At the same time, it was reassuring to realize that they didn't see me any differently. I was always afraid that if people knew the truth, they'd assume I was deeply insecure and view me as a victim. Ultimately, I feared that in their eyes my mom's abuse would detract from my positive qualities and make people question who I really was. It was comforting to know that Lisa and Reanne had faith in me.

Over the next month or so, I met with Lisa and Reanne regularly, sharing more each time. Then on a warm April day I was at the YMCA playing basketball by myself. As I was about to take a shot, I heard my phone ring. I looked down and saw that I had several missed calls, all from my mom. I picked up the phone, my heart pounding, and braced myself as I dialed. I knew that whatever it was, it was bad. But when my mother picked up the phone she said nothing. There was complete silence for about thirty seconds, and then she said in a perfectly calm and proper voice, "Zachary, Child Protective Services is here. Please come home as soon as you can."

I hung up and called Reanne. She had told me to call her anytime, but it went straight to her voice mail. Not knowing what else to do, I jumped on my bike and headed home.

When I got there, my mother was sitting in the living room with Kevin, who had a blank look on his face, and two women from CPS. My mother was acting like the Queen of England — complimenting their shoes and offering them lemonade. I had seen this before. She could turn on the charm with ease when she wanted to. "Hi, Zachary," one of the women said. "We'd like to ask you a few questions about living with your mom."

To this day, I cannot for the life of me understand why they questioned me in front of her. My mother had intimidated me since I was a toddler. I was absolutely terrified. Of course I lied, and I made sure to lie well. "She is a wonderful mother, and I am proud to be her son," I told them.

They went on to ask specific questions that clearly revealed I had told somebody something: "Has your mother ever talked about castrating your father? Did she hit you with a flyswatter when you were younger? Has she ever forcefully berated you?" I denied all of it. Not only that, but I convinced them it wasn't true.

"No," I told them emphatically, using all the body language techniques my mom had drilled into me. "She has never done any of that." My heart was pounding. I was sure they could tell how nervous I was, but I did my best to stay composed.

The entire time, my mom sat there looking calm and poised. At one point, she even offered to leave the room, but the women said that wasn't necessary. Finally, they thanked my mom and asked if it was possible for me to stay with another family member until the investigation was over. My mom agreed right away and called Lola to come pick me up.

Since we'd moved to the suburbs, Lola now lived almost an hour away. I quickly realized that these women were going to leave before she got there. Inside, I began to panic as they shook my mother's hand and told her again what a pleasure it had been to meet her. They walked outside and got into their car as my mother stood by the front door and watched them. I stayed in my seat, petrified.

When their car pulled away, my mom closed and locked the door and walked toward me. Then she pulled her chair right up next to mine and sat beside me, staring at me. The tip of her nose was maybe three inches away from my cheek. She glared at me for several minutes, and then, as if she were talking to herself, she said, "I have always been a wonderful mother to you, Zachary."

Before long, Lola knocked on the door. Before she got up, my mom leaned in even closer to me and stared at me for another minute, this time looking me up and down from head to toe. Then she got up, unlocked the door, and went into her bedroom without saying a word.

I went up to my room to get my things. I didn't know how long I'd be at Lola's house, so I only packed what I needed for school and a few clothes. Then I went back downstairs. As we were about to leave, I heard my mother call out to me from her room, "You better not leave without giving me a hug." I walked back to her room. She grabbed me and held me against her for a good thirty seconds. "I have always done my best by you, Zachary," she told me. "I have always been a wonderful mother." And then she let me go.

From the moment I got in Lola's car, we couldn't talk about anything except how this had happened. "I told your mother she had to stop doing some of that stuff," she muttered as she drove. "Maybe a neighbor heard something. Or did you tell somebody something?" I told her that I hadn't. At that point, I didn't know how much I could trust Lola. Our relationship had changed since I was a little boy, and I'd never forgotten how she'd ultimately abandoned me after I'd confided in her about my mom years before.

Lola and my mom had always had a complicated relationship. When they were fighting, which was often, Lola stood up for me. But when she and my mom were getting along, she enabled, defended, and excused my mom's worst behavior. Now she wavered between supporting me and castigating me for not being a good enough son.

Papa was out of town visiting family, so it was just Lola and me. Over the next few days, I told Lola more and more of the truth. She looked traumatized when I told her some of the things my mom had said and done. We both knew that CPS was going to interview me again, and Lola told me over and over that I would have to lie. "We've got to think this through," she told me. "You don't want your mom to go to jail. Use that good brain of yours to come up with a reason that she did those things." Finally Lola told me to say that I thought I had an STD, so I'd asked my mom to look at me. When I hesitated, she threatened, "You want a place to sleep, don't you?"

I was furious at Lola. But mostly I felt so

alone. At her house, I was an hour away from Roeper. I made that commute on public transportation each day, worrying that my mom would appear around every corner. For the first time, I couldn't concentrate at school. I was too worried about what would happen next and afraid that I'd look out the window and see my mom staring back at me. Besides Reanne, who had her own family to worry about, I had no one to turn to. If this all caved in, what was going to happen to me?

After just a few days, Lola took me to a sad-looking facility for my second interview with CPS. When we were in the car on the way there, my phone rang. It was my mom. "Let me be perfectly clear," she said calmly. "You know what you have to do. And you will do it." Then she hung up.

Inside, I went through interview after grueling interview with different people. One after another, they asked me a series of questions. "Has your mother ever threatened to knock your head through a back window? Has your mother ever beaten you with an instrument? Has your mother ever spoken to you about sex in an inappropriate way?" Every specific thing they asked was true, but I denied it all.

As soon as I was done, I panicked. I re-

120

alized that I was going to have to go back to my mom and that I was going to be made to suffer greatly. I had done the unthinkable. I had talked. And that had caused these people to go into my mother's home and question her very competency as a parent. I knew my mother well enough to know that someone, almost definitely me, was going to have to pay for that. I couldn't go back there.

I tried talking to my dad and telling him that I wished I could go live with him. He would never turn me away, but he knew how hard things would be for me in DC and didn't want me to have to start over at a new school when I was doing so well at Roeper. He wasn't about to start a custody battle with my mom just to put me in what he saw as a worse situation than the one I was already in.

But I saw it differently. I went to Reanne a few days later and said, "I need to talk to them again so I can tell the truth, but it needs to be somewhere I'm comfortable talking." Within an hour or two, one of the women from CPS showed up at Roeper, and I finally told her the truth. I didn't want my mom to go to jail, so I told her enough to get me out of there. I knew what was enough. In that interview, I said that I wanted to go live with my dad.

Within days, CPS made an official recommendation for me to move in with him. When I called him and said, "It looks like I'll be coming down there," his response was simply, "All right, cool."

The school year was almost over, and I'd been looking forward to my eighth-grade class trip to Chicago all year. I was at the train station with all my friends, about to get on the train, when my science teacher ran up and said, "Zach, you can't go." I didn't understand what was going on. "Your mom called and said you can't go." My friends were boarding the train, some of them calling my name to join them, when I realized that she'd done this on purpose.

It took Lola an hour to come and get me, so I had to wait there with my science teacher's husband, watching the train pull away. I was heated. But even then, I heard my mother's words in my head about being a black man in America and never showing anger, so I held it together and chatted politely with my teacher's husband until Lola picked me up.

Right after the trip was my eighth-grade graduation. All my friends were excited about the summer and starting high school in the fall, but I had a sinking feeling inside.

122

I knew all the challenges I'd be facing in DC and felt I had nothing to look forward to. Before I left, Reanne arranged for a police officer to accompany us to my house so I could get my things. I made sure to go at a time when my mom and Kevin wouldn't be home.

After the police officer checked the house to make sure no one was there, I went inside to my room, expecting to find it the way I'd left it just a few weeks before. Instead, everything was gone. My closet, which had been full of clothes, was empty. Books were scattered across the floor, many with their pages ripped out. A trophy I'd earned from a forensics competition back at GPA was lying on my bed, snapped in half.

When I left for DC, I didn't even have a suitcase. I had a backpack with two outfits in it and the clothes I was wearing, half of which belonged to Papa. The day before I got on the plane, my mother texted me. "I'm driving up to the house, and you're going to come outside and get in the car," she said.

"No, Mom," I responded. "I'm not going to do that." It was the first time I'd directly disobeyed my mom. I didn't know what would happen to me if I got in that car, and I did not want to find out. I wanted her to know that she couldn't control me anymore.

Yet in some ways, of course, she still did. I hated that she still had an effect on me, whether it was my fear that she'd show up at an unexpected moment — even after I arrived in DC — or my visceral reaction to certain words or phrases she used, or the way I second-guessed my posture and body language, knowing that if she were there she would find a way to criticize me for some small perceived infraction.

As I've grown older, I've come to understand and even appreciate the fact that I've gained a lot of positive attributes from my experiences with my mother — including my resilience, my speaking skills, and my ability to understand and connect with so many people. But as I boarded that plane, I desperately wanted to erase the memory of every moment I'd spent with her. For a moment, I even wished that I had no fear of death, because then I could have killed myself to terminate the effect she had had on me.

CHAPTER 4
STARTING OVER AGAIN

My grandmother's house was in Bellevue, a small neighborhood in Ward 8, which was well-known as the poorest ward in Washington, DC. When I was living in Detroit with my mom, poverty, crime, and violence were present in the community, but as long as I rode my bike in one direction from our condo, I could usually avoid seeing them up close. Plus, poverty was not nearly as concentrated in my former Detroit community as it was in the part of DC my grandma lived in. Now my home was in the center of a neighborhood where looking at the wrong person the wrong way could get you killed.

My biggest fear when moving to DC was that I would have to go to the local high school, Ballou. Every once in a while, there was a report on the news about a shooting at Ballou. There were metal detectors at the entrances, scant resources, and few opportunities there for real learning. It was a dead end, and I knew that, coming from a liberal private school environment like Roeper to a rough inner-city school like Ballou, I would be a target. I was pretty good at code switching by then, and as I walked the streets of my new neighborhood I got better and better at fitting in among the other guys my age, but I knew I'd never be able to fit in at Ballou. I knew how to carry myself in a way that made it easier for me to blend in, but I wasn't hard. If I went to Ballou, I'd be asking to get jumped, ridiculed, or worse.

So my focus when moving to DC was on getting into a good school. But it was summer by then, and at that point most schools were fully enrolled for the coming year. Many even had long wait lists. Luckily, Randall Dunn, the headmaster from Roeper, was a huge help and put me in touch with the administrations at some of the best schools in the area. I was accepted at all of them, but several had no choice but to place me on the wait list. At one school, an administrator even implied during my interview that they had to put another kid ahead of me on the wait list because of who his parents were.

To get to those interviews, I had to take

public transportation. For the first year and a half that I was living in DC, my dad rarely had a car. When he did, it was in poor condition and usually broke down shortly after he got it. Having to walk or take the bus everywhere made me feel exposed. It forced me to be in close proximity to and interact with intimidating people who in Detroit I would have just driven by with my mom. In our neighborhood, for every relatively quiet street like mine, there were one or two that were rowdier, full of groups of guys hanging out on the corner or in front of a liquor store. When I walked through and around these groups, I tried to fix my stance, my posture, and my face so that I would look like I belonged or at least not stand out quite so much.

One night early in the summer, I was coming home from one of my interviews. After taking the Metro to Anacostia, the closest stop, which was more than two miles from my house, I waited for the bus that would bring me closer to home. It didn't come. I overheard someone at the station say that there had been a shooting and they had temporarily shut down the bus line. After waiting for two hours, I decided to walk.

Until then, I had walked within only a

five- or six-block radius of my house. Now, walking for more than thirty minutes from Anacostia in the dark, I was afraid. I was wearing a suit and tie for the interview and carrying a backpack, and I was well aware of how much I stood out. Block after block, I walked quickly, but not so fast that I appeared scared, as I passed abandoned buildings, a few homeless people and drug addicts, and mostly groups of people hanging out on street corners. On one block, two guys were fighting in the center of a circle of onlookers. I did my best to stay out of everyone's way. Sometimes I crisscrossed the same street several times to avoid groups of people.

As I walked past one corner store, I noticed a group of guys sitting on the stoop outside. "Hey, li'l nigga," I heard one guy call out. My heart sank. I knew he was talking to me, but I wasn't sure how to respond. What would he do if I turned around and approached him? What would he do if I ran? In the back of my head, I was thinking that at some point, I'd have to make this walk again. So if I ran now it would be even more difficult the next time. "I know you hear me, nigga. Come over here for a second, let me holler at you right quick."

I turned and walked over to him. "What

you lookin' all scared for?" he asked me. He seemed to be high or drunk or both. He mumbled to himself for a minute and then said, "Lemme hold a dollar right quick."

"Sorry, boss, I don't have anything," I told him. His face froze, and then he stood up. He was taller than I'd thought, at least three or four inches taller than me. "Lemme tell you something, li'l nigga," he said seriously, curving his body so that he was leaning slightly over me. "You can't let these niggas punk you, man. You just walked over to me. You don't have to get all close like that."

I took a breath as I realized that this guy wasn't trying to throw hands or take advantage of me. In fact, he was trying to help me by explaining everything that I'd done wrong. He told me to keep my distance from people and loosen my grip on my backpack so I didn't appear scared. For the rest of my walk, I took his advice, and when I finally got home, I was exhausted.

The people who lived on the quieter streets in Bellevue like mine were mostly older, working-class blacks like my grandmother, who'd made a living as a janitor and janitorial supervisor for decades. Others were more highly educated black professionals like our neighbor Ms. Brown, who was in her late sixties and still worked as a substitute teacher at a high school in Bethesda, Maryland. I often saw Ms. Brown around the neighborhood — on the bus or walking to get groceries. She was a kind and very smart woman who took a liking to me and always called me "Mr. President."

Whenever I saw her carrying bags of groceries or walking home from the bus stop at night, I helped Ms. Brown to her door. The first few times I did this, she tried to pay me, but I refused. After a while, she told me, "I will only let you keep helping me if you accept the money," and I relented.

As we rode the bus together and during those walks home, Ms. Brown and I had long talks about everything from the history of the neighborhood to politics and current events. Often these topics intersected. Ms. Brown had lived in Bellevue for thirty years. As we rode past dilapidated and boarded-up buildings, she told me, "This used to be such a nice shopping center. I was usually the only black woman who went there."

"What happened?" I asked her.

"A lot of things," she told me. She explained that until the 1960s, Bellevue and nearby Anacostia were mostly white, working-class neighborhoods. Many of the people who lived there worked across the Anacostia River in the Navy Yard. Then, in the 1960s, the city built the Anacostia Freeway, which separated Anacostia from the waterfront, and put up several public housing projects near the freeway. As many of the middle-class whites fled to the suburbs, development in the area slowed. Then existing businesses moved out during the crack era of the 1980s and early '90s. And as the mass incarceration of blacks, particularly black men, continued to rise, families were broken apart, opportunities and conveniences grew even scarcer, and a sense of hopelessness and resentment took over.

I had already read many books about these issues and was grateful to have someone like her to talk to about them. We spent a lot of time discussing Cornel West's book *Race Matters* and his concept of black nihilism. West argues that the lack of hope, meaning, and love in black communities leads to a cold-hearted mentality that is both individually self-destructive and damaging to black communities. This was the best and most frequently missing explanation for the way people in my neighborhood felt and acted, and it resonated deeply with me. Hearing Ms. Brown's explanation of our neighborhood's history helped me see it even more clearly.

I knew how lucky I was to have found a

131

path toward upward mobility, and it was obvious to me that nearly every time that happened to someone like me, it was because of specific exceptional circumstances that had provided a way out. For me, it was having a mother who, despite her many flaws, valued education and my ability to hold a conversation; grandparents who had traveled the world and were educators and child psychologists; and a father who was willing to sacrifice nearly everything to give me opportunities he'd never had.

Without them, my life would likely have been just like the other kids' in Bellevue. I could have had a dad in prison, a mom who was desperately trying to make it and didn't have the time or energy to give me love and support, and teachers who were sick and tired of my black ass and just wanted me to sit down and be quiet. The drugs, the violence, and the hostility — that was years of oppression and accumulated disadvantages coming out. I knew where that came from. Despite my relative advantages, I felt it every day. But I was also determined to make the most of my unique opportunities and hopefully use them one day to make a difference. And I could do that only by avoiding the traps that were laid at every turn for me and all the other kids like me.

So when I wasn't working on my applications or taking public transportation to interviews, I was alone in the house, reading. My dad was rarely around because he was always working. At that point, he had three jobs. His first and main source of employment was working as an accounts-payable coordinator at Business Software Alliance. He'd been working there for six years. When he left there every day at five, he went to work as a valet until about midnight. Then he delivered newspapers from one to four in the morning before finally heading home and sleeping for a couple of hours. Then he'd wake up and start all over again.

My grandma Pearl was in a similar situation. She had been working two jobs — as a janitor and a janitorial supervisor — for twenty-six years. For most of her life, my grandmother had been able to support her modest lifestyle. Then, in the years before I moved to DC, her health declined, her diabetes medication made her gain weight, and it became harder and harder for her to get around, work, and keep the house in decent shape. She could barely walk up the stairs; there were dark stains on the wall where she had to pause and lean her shoulder as she slowly worked her way up.

The rest of the house was in bad shape, too. It had never been much; the entire house consisted of a tiny, cramped living room; a small dining area that was completely taken up by a four-person table; a galley kitchen; and two little bedrooms and one bathroom upstairs. The basement had flooded and was now full of mildew, so we couldn't use it as a living space or even keep many of our things down there. Instead, everyone's belongings were scattered throughout the cramped house — one corner of the living room held an ironing board, a bicycle, and piles of old clothes. The bathroom upstairs was stained from all the times my grandmother couldn't get up the stairs quickly enough. There were holes in the kitchen floor that we had patched with plywood and a huge hole in the ceiling of the second bedroom.

That hole in the ceiling became the bane of my existence during my years in DC. We were constantly trying to patch it with new drywall or cover it with garbage bags to keep out vermin and stop the water from leaking into the house when it rained, but nothing we did ever fixed the root problem, which was a faulty roof. Of course it would have been best to just repair or replace the roof itself, but we didn't have the money for that.

So no matter how many times we patched and repainted that ceiling, fresh water damage appeared every time it rained. It took only a few rainstorms to create another hole. That leak in the roof became a symbol to me of what it was like to live in poverty. No matter what we did to try to fix it, there was always a deeper, more insidious problem at the heart of it, causing more and more damage.

My father was working three jobs and had been for years. And his main source of income wasn't a minimum-wage job. As an accounts-payable coordinator, he was a skilled white-collar worker. The income from that job alone should have been enough to support at least a modest lifestyle, but it wasn't.

The thing that most people who have never lived in poverty don't understand is how expensive it is to be poor. Making the minimum payments on everything from credit card bills to medical expenses causes interest to add up exponentially. Even something like my braces cost so much more in the long run because we couldn't afford to pay for them up front. I had gotten braces back in sixth grade, but the process ended up taking twice as long as it should have — and costing even more than that — because I never went to my appointments consistently to keep things moving forward on schedule. My mom had set up a payment plan with my original orthodontist in Michigan, and my dad had given her extra child support to pay for it, but she often took that money to the casino.

Instead of going every month as I was supposed to, because we didn't have the money, I went to the orthodontist only maybe two or three times between sixth and eighth grade. And since I had gone so long in between adjustments, several of my front teeth had been pulled too far in one direction. When I got to DC I had to find a new orthodontist, and when he looked at my teeth, he was concerned. "What have you been doing?" he asked me. "These braces can really mess up your teeth if you don't do this right." He had to basically start the process over from the beginning and create a new plan to get my teeth back in line, which would take another eighteen months.

We set up a new payment plan, which of course would accrue plenty of interest, and set up weekly appointments to get everything back on track. I showed up every week and swiped my card, and it was rejected about half the time because there wasn't enough money. Sometimes the orthodontist took pity on me and saw me anyway, but most of the time he didn't.

Pulling my top teeth in one direction and then back in the other left a gap almost the size of two teeth on the right side. Eventually I would need an implant to fill in that empty space. So now, to make more room for the implant, the orthodontist was trying to create an even bigger gap. I was so embarrassed by this. It wasn't like having a gap in between my two front teeth, which plenty of people have. It was off center and huge — it looked like I was missing a tooth, which essentially I was. People commented on it often, and it was always in the back of my mind. When I was talking to people, I would hold my mouth in a certain way so the gap would be less noticeable.

This caused me so much anxiety, and the financial aspect was a huge source of stress for my dad. It was a bill we constantly had to pay but could never afford. I just wanted to get the entire process over with, and every time my card got rejected I knew we were driving up the cost and pushing the end date back further and further. To make things even worse, my mom had never paid off the orthodontist in Michigan and had put that bill in my dad's name. So as we struggled to pay the new doctor, my dad was still trying to find a way to pay the old one.

Then there were things that ate away at my dad's income that had nothing to do with socioeconomics — namely, my mom. When they were married, my mom would take my dad's credit card and go on huge shopping sprees, buying furniture and other things we couldn't afford. They'd also held a lavish wedding that they'd paid for mostly with credit cards. When I moved to DC, my dad had just finally managed to get out of credit card debt. For more than ten years, he'd also been paying for my child support plus all the extras that my mom demanded, most of which she spent at the casino. Since he'd split up with Brenda, he was also paying child support for Nicole, but because they shared custody, that was in addition to all the expenses he was responsible for during the times when Nicole was with him.

Despite all these hardships and challenges, my father had always found a way to pay for my private school tuition. After my scholarship, his portion came to about a thousand dollars a month. I was well aware of how many fathers in his position would have just refused to pay that bill. I would have had no choice but to go to public school. But ever since he'd attended Dads'

Day at GPA, my dad believed in the value of that education. He felt that a quality education was the only thing he could give me that would open doors and ensure I got ahead. He didn't have the connections or money to open those doors, so he was willing to work three jobs, go without a car, and sacrifice many, many small comforts so that he could give that to me.

He was determined to do the same thing for Nicole. Like me, she stayed in her public school until third grade and then switched to a private school in Virginia. Nicole was very smart, although not as academically ambitious as me, and had always been a sensitive kid. My dad wanted to give her every possible advantage, so he paid for the portion of her tuition that her scholarship didn't cover as well as the cost of her ballet class and music lessons.

This is yet another reason that being from a disadvantaged area is so expensive. If I had lived in a neighborhood with better schools — either in DC or back in Michigan — it would have been no problem for me to go to the local school. But because we lived where we did, the choice was either to go to a school with a startling lack of resources or find a way to pay for a better education. This is precisely why private schools that have wealthy donors, influential alumni, and prodigious endowments should offer more generous financial aid. Many private schools care about diversity because it is promotional, makes them look good, and allows them to say that an education at their school will expose students to a variety of perspectives and backgrounds. However, many of these same schools care more about their endowments and reputations than diversity and the hardships faced by disadvantaged minority students who attend their institutions.

Working to pay for my private school education meant that life outside of school was rough. There were now five people living in that tiny two-bedroom house: Me, my grandma, my dad, my uncle Lee, and, half the time, Nicole. Lee had been living there for years, so the second bedroom was his. Lee was a good uncle, and I enjoyed hanging out with him. He was a faithful Christian who worked as a security guard at his church and at the airport and had an upbeat personality. Lee had never lived on his own and didn't know how to use certain technology, so when my dad was at work, it fell on me to help him. I was happy to help, but without a computer or other resources at home, it was challenging.

If I wanted to print something out for Lee or type up an essay for a school application, I had to walk six blocks to the local library, where there were only three computers. Usually there would be a homeless guy at one, a group of kids hanging out by the other, and a student trying to do his or her work at the third. I just had to stand there and wait until one of them got up. This often didn't happen until the library closed, and then I had to walk home and beg my dad to let me go to work with him in the morning to use his computer.

With Lee and my grandma in the two bedrooms, my dad slept on the small couch in the living room, and I slept on a cot next to him. My dad is six feet two, and the couch was small — maybe five feet long. I hated seeing my dad scrunched up on that thing after working so hard every day. But I wasn't much better off on the cot. It had been strong enough for me to sleep on back when I was a kid and visited for a month or so at a time, but it broke under my weight after I'd been living in DC for only a few weeks. From then on, I just slept on the floor. Often, my dad would offer to switch places, but I told him I was fine.

When Nicole was with us, she slept with my grandma, which she hated. Nicole was getting older and more aware of the differences between life at her mom's comfortable condo and life at my dad's house. But she was still too young to understand the reasons behind those differences or how painful it was to our dad when she pointed them out. One day shortly after I moved in, she was upset about something and started complaining.

"I don't like sleeping with Grandma," she told my dad. "There are stains on the sheets and the bathroom is always so dirty. It looks like someone peed and went number two on the carpet." I looked at my dad as he sat there listening to all this. I knew that Nicole didn't mean any harm; she was just a kid, and she didn't realize the impact of her words. But I wished she'd somehow register the pain on my dad's face and stop talking. He was working so hard and doing everything he could for us, and his facial expression told me exactly what it felt like to hear his daughter tell him that it still wasn't enough.

I've spent a lot of time trying to understand my dad. Because he's so reserved, the things he's done for other people have told me far more about the man he is than anything he's said to me. I may not have been aware of it at the time, but when I got to DC, I needed someone to talk to. After everything I'd just been through — the abuse, the fear, the confessions, and the pain of having to leave home and start over again under very tough circumstances — I had no emotional support, no one to help me process it and figure out the right way to move on. CPS had completely disappeared after making their recommendation for me to move to DC.

My dad was the most likely candidate to give me emotional support, but whenever I tried to open up to him, I got one-sentence answers at best. So I quickly stopped trying. It would have been easy for me to assume that my father simply couldn't relate to anything I'd been through, but the more I've learned about his background, the more I've realized that the opposite is true.

I never met my dad's father, my grandfather, but from the stories I've heard from relatives, my impression of him is of a smart guy with great social skills and a remarkable memory. My grandmother always described him to me as a great talker. "He was like you, Zachary," she told me. "He could talk to anyone about anything."

Despite his positive qualities, my grandfather, after a brief stint in the military, became a reckless and violent alcoholic who

143

was in and out of jail the rest of his life. When he was around, which throughout my dad's childhood was rare, he abused my grandmother and was violent with my dad and his two brothers. According to one story I heard several times, he once threw my uncle down the steps when he was just a toddler sitting in his stroller. Fortunately, my dad caught the stroller before it hit the wall at the bottom. When he was absent from their lives, my grandmother struggled to support her three sons by working as a waitress, so she sent them to live with her parents.

From then on, my father had no consistent parental presence in his life. He saw his dad only once every few years. His mom visited him more frequently, but there were several times when she said she was coming to see him and then got stuck working or couldn't afford the trip and failed to show up. When I heard this, I realized it was why, no matter what, my dad always made sure to make the drive to Michigan to see me when he said he would. One time it was snowing so badly that his car got stuck and he couldn't continue. That's the only time he didn't make it, and I knew he'd tried.

My dad learned early on to lower his expectations for people and swallow his emotions. I've never once heard him complain about anything. Not his childhood, not the disadvantages he's faced, and not how hard he's had to work for so little.

For a long time I just assumed that nothing bothered him, but as I've struggled to embrace vulnerability in my own life, I've begun to wonder how much he's internalized the hyper-masculine idea of what it means to be a "real nigga." Our society is one that discourages men from showing too much emotion. For black men, who have been degraded and oppressed, from the time of slavery to Jim Crow–era lynching and today's police brutality and mass incarceration, any sign of vulnerability or weakness takes on another level of significance, almost like an added layer of resistance. In the black community, men usually don't go to therapy or talk about how difficult their childhoods were. They man up, act hard, move forward, and do what they have to to survive. And that's exactly what my dad has done, seemingly without any resentment or hostility toward his father or anyone else who contributed to the difficulties of his childhood.

When my dad was in his twenties, his father was nearing the end of his life. Despite the fact that his father had never been there for him, until the day he died, my dad visited him every other day to spend time with him, clean his house, and even prepare his food. When my dad's older brother battled his own addiction and psychological issues, my father sacrificed to pay for him to go to rehab and later to have a place to stay. He has always been there for the people he cares about, and he was there for me, too, though maybe not in the exact way I needed at the time.

In that house in DC, I was lonely. I didn't have any friends in my neighborhood, because I wasn't like most of the boys who hung out on my block. I woke up every day, afraid that my mom would catch me off guard and seek vengeance. I told my dad to be careful when he was out. My mom had made so many violent threats against him over the years, and I wondered if she'd now follow through. "Oh, you don't have to tell me," he told me. "My head is always on a swivel."

I was almost relieved when he got home safely from work, though it was usually in the early morning. During the day, all I did was read and write in my journal as a way of processing some of my experiences. My happiest moments were when I took a break to play with Nicole.

That summer, it was sweltering outside, as it was in the house. We had no air-conditioning or way of cooling off, and that stifled energy mirrored the way I felt inside. I was angry and frustrated, often wanting to pop off or punch something. But I was also determined to avoid that trap.

When I was finally accepted at the Bullis School, a prep school in Potomac, Maryland, I was more determined than ever to turn this fresh start into something positive by making lasting friendships and proving my worth to everyone I encountered there. I knew it would be a challenge. Bullis was an hour's drive from the house, which meant it would take more than two hours each way using public transportation. And we could afford to buy only two sets of the school uniform, which I would have to wash by hand. We didn't have a washing machine or a dryer, and the closest laundromat was a long walk or bus ride away.

But I wasn't afraid of hard work, lack of sleep, or doing whatever it took to succeed at Bullis. I'd channel all my anger and frustration into doing more and being more than I ever had before. For the first time, I could focus on achieving without the threat of my mom showing up and ruining it for me. I could make friends without her infecting those relationships with her projections and overreactions. I could even be a "normal" teenager and date without it being tainted by my mom's warped ideas about sex.

At least, that was my plan. It didn't end up working out that way at all.

CHAPTER 5
COMEBACK ROUTE

On my first day at Bullis, I was asleep on the living room floor when my alarm went off at 4:45 a.m. I quickly shut it off, hoping not to wake up my dad, who had gotten home from work just an hour before. I stretched my body out on the ground and forced myself to get up. It was still dark outside, and I had a long day ahead of me.

When I left the house soon after, the sun was just starting to rise, casting a slight glow on the small, barren lots that filled my neighborhood. As I walked to the bus stop, I heard a dog barking. At first I assumed it was coming from behind one of the chain-link fences that lined the sidewalk. Then, as I crossed the street, a dog came charging down the road toward me. He looked rabid and malnourished. I quickly hopped up on top of a parked car to avoid him and stayed there until he moved on.

From then on, I made no assumptions.

When I heard a dog barking, I quickly scanned the block to see if any loose dogs were out and, if so, what my quickest form of escape would be. I learned to stay circumspect and proceed with caution every time I passed a car, ready to run or react swiftly in case someone or something jumped out at me.

At the bus stop, I pulled a book out of my backpack and waited. Pretty much the only other people out at that time were homeless. Some of them were sleeping; others mumbled to themselves or to me. I would have stood out no matter what I was wearing, but I was in my prep school uniform — an easy target. I remembered everything I'd learned from Yeti, the guys on the basketball court in my old neighborhood in Detroit, and my earlier walks through the neighborhood. I tried to lean my body a little and tilt my head to evoke a certain masculine strength.

"You got that tie on, nigga," one guy mumbled to me, reaching out his hand. "Lemme hold that tie for a minute." I didn't reply, hoping he would give up and move on, but instead he got mad. "What the fuck is up with you, nigga?" he asked, stumbling a little as he walked toward me. "You a wannabe-white-ass nigga."

I tried to defuse these situations and play it cool, but, depending on whom I was dealing with, that could be difficult. When the bus pulled up a minute later, I was hoping this dude wouldn't get on behind me. Luckily, he didn't that time. But the bus was filled with people facing any number of challenges. There were folks who were loud and obnoxious, irritable and grumpy, depressed and detached from reality, and others who were just pissed, ready to pop off and raise hell over the slightest thing, like my backpack brushing their shoulder as I walked to the back of the bus to sit down.

I took a seat and continued reading, trying to avoid eye contact with some of the angrier-looking faces that surrounded me. After a few more stops, a guy got on the bus who looked like he could bench-press a small car. He was tall with dreads, with no shirt on and tattoos all over his body. It was clear from the moment he stepped on the bus that he was having a bad day.

"I'm gonna kill all these niggas, yo, don't fuck with me!" As he made his way past me to the back of the bus, he kicked the empty seats and punched some of the windows. I quickly put my book away and changed the expression on my face so that I looked a little tougher and slightly angry — but not so much that it would attract his attention. Then, from behind me I heard him say, "Yo, li'l nigga, get up."

No matter how many situations like this I'd dealt with, I still wasn't sure how to respond. If I ignored him, I'd be asking for a confrontation, but if I got up, I'd be admitting weakness. For a moment, I stayed in my seat, and then I saw him coming toward me out of the corners of my eyes, bumping into the seats and pushing people out of his way. "Oh, I'm about to whup your bitch ass," he threatened. I stood up. "Yeah, that's right," he said, taking my seat.

"Yo, man, I don't want any trouble," I said. My goal was to comply calmly without seeming submissive or afraid.

"I ain't fuckin' with these li'l niggas, Moe, I ain't playin' with 'em. You feel me?"

"Aye no disrespect, boss, I hear you," I said. Fortunately, that was enough to keep him from kicking my ass.

The commute was challenging, but moments like these helped me build an understanding of how to navigate drastically different environments and communicate with people from those different backgrounds. I found that sometimes code switching was about fitting in and making myself seem more familiar and therefore more likable.

Other times, it was about avoiding danger, concealing fear, and preventing confrontations from escalating and leaving me with a black eye. I saw that it was not enough merely to try to talk to people, no matter how genuine my desire to connect with them may have been. What mattered was my ability to understand the world they were coming from and the codes of behavior they lived by.

It would have been easy for me to think of this guy as a thug, a prime example of a big, scary, angry black man who spent most of his time on the streets contributing to the crime, violence, and fear in poor black communities. It would have been easy to assume that this guy probably had no job; was a poor father, if he was one; and called the women he slept around with "slim-thick bitches" and "hos with phat asses." But when I thought about my experiences and all that I'd read, I realized that thinking about this guy as some sort of pathological menace was a convenient way of avoiding how all of us were implicated in the aspects of his experience that we distort.

All this happened just on the bus ride to my first stop, Anacostia station. After getting on the Metro at Anacostia, I switched lines twice before getting on another bus

153

that took me to Bullis. That final leg of my journey could not have been any more different from the first ride of the day. Within the span of one daily commute, I'd gone from the worst part of the inner city to Potomac, Maryland, the town that CNN listed that same year as one of the most affluent in the country. I looked out of the bus window as we passed huge homes surrounded by acres of land and perfectly manicured lawns.

I'd seen big homes before, but the magnitude of these mansions blew my mind. Potomac was like Grosse Pointe on steroids. These weren't houses; they were manors. Some of them had majestic fountains on their front lawns. Others looked like replicas of European castles that had been outfitted with every modern convenience. The one word that echoed through my mind as I looked out of the bus window was *power.*

By this time, I understood far more about the world of wealth and privilege than I did back when I was first exposed to it at GPA. Now I knew exactly whom I'd be going to school with — the children of real estate tycoons and magnates, representatives and senators, the country's social and political elite. Of course, not every kid at Bullis came from that background. Some students were there on athletic scholarships. Others came from more modest families. But I was pretty sure that few if any of them had a background quite like mine. So I started at Bullis wanting to stand out and make a statement about who I was before they could form any preconceived notions about me.

Part of this was my natural competitive drive, but a piece of it came from not wanting to be lumped in with the black kids who were recruited to Bullis to play sports or who were just there to "add diversity." I wanted to prove that I added something even more valuable.

But on my first day I didn't have time to think about any of that. I was too busy trying to find my way. I'd gotten a list of school supplies that I was supposed to bring with me, but I hadn't been able to get any of them. I hated asking my dad for money to buy that stuff. I'd seen how much just buying the school uniform had stretched our budget, and it was costing an additional $350 a month just for me to get to school on the Metro.

Even getting to the store to buy school supplies was a challenge. It wasn't as if my mom or dad was going to just buy them for me. Like so many other responsibilities that were taken care of by the parents of most of my peers, getting school supplies fell to me. The CVS in Bellevue was poorly stocked, and the closest Kmart was three miles away. It was a big-time commitment to take the bus there or walk, and I had so much to keep tabs on at home. Every morning, I had to spray the furniture and appliances where there tended to be ant infestations, scour the floor for crumbs to avoid attracting rodents, and check the basement to make sure the kitchen sink hadn't leaked down there.

The last thing I wanted to do was worry about traveling three miles by myself to buy school supplies. I thought I'd just figure it out. But the pens I'd grabbed at home before leaving for school that morning were mostly out of ink or didn't write well, and I had only one notebook to use for all my classes. This wasn't how I wanted to begin my first day at a new school — already behind. I tried to find the lost-and-found to see if there was anything there I could use, but I didn't know where it was. Finally, I knocked on the door to a teacher's office and asked her if I could borrow a few pens.

In class, I paid close attention to the class dynamic, feeling out the other students and teachers alike. Who were they? What mattered to them? And why? On the first day, I was so focused on learning the ropes socially that I couldn't concentrate in class as much as I would have liked. I was distracted by other thoughts, too. In my English class, we went around and shared thoughts about the summer reading, and when it was my turn, I had lost focus because I was wondering if my mom knew where I was and if she was plotting her revenge against me.

I had decided to play football that year, so I stayed after school for practice. I had never played football before, but I felt a strong desire to throw myself completely into something new and challenging. I also thought it would be a good way to make friends, a way to find the sense of belonging I was looking for. On the football field, it felt good to push myself to the point of exhaustion, until it hurt, to get hit hard and have no choice but to get back up.

Before school started, my dad had asked me why I wanted to play football. I told him I thought it would be a cool challenge. But there was more to it than that. My dad was a good athlete in high school. His best sport was basketball, but he decided to play football his senior year, too. He had been tall, with broad shoulders and a muscular physique since middle school, and he'd always enjoyed playing sports far more than any of his classes. Though basketball was his favorite sport to play, football was his favorite sport to watch, he'd say. He watched football every Sunday. It was probably the only thing he ever did regularly for himself. And even though I wasn't as interested in football as he was, I'd tried to watch games with him when I had time.

But I didn't play football because I thought my dad would be able to come to most of my games. And I didn't play because I thought I'd be a high school phenom. To me, my dad was like iron. Despite my mom's efforts, when I looked at my father, I saw a man who buried emotion, resisted vulnerability, and did everything he could to provide for his family. I wanted to be as strong as he was. I wanted to endure without complaint, to prove to him that I could bleed without needing a Band-Aid. I wanted my dad to be proud of me. To see that I would put every fiber of my being into something that mattered to him far more than any book I was reading over the weekend.

I had always been athletic, but it turned out I wasn't a good football player. I'd thought that my intellectual skills and natural athleticism would automatically translate to the football field, but that wasn't happening. I'd been practicing with the team since the preseason had started late in the summer, but I was still having a hard time following the plays and understanding the terminology. That day, I didn't get any playing time, and I was frustrated by my own lack of skill.

By the time football practice was over, it was evening, and I made my commute back home again in the dark. When I got home at nine o'clock, the house was empty. Both my dad and grandma were still at work, and Lee was probably at church. I dropped my backpack on the couch and made my way into the kitchen, carefully stepping over the plywood that covered the hole in the floor. The fridge was mostly empty. In a cabinet, I found a box of crackers, so I grabbed that and ate them as I gathered my grandmother's dirty laundry, took off my uniform, and brought them downstairs.

We didn't have a washing machine, so we washed our clothes by hand in the basement sink. My dad usually handled this for my grandma, but he'd be at work for most of the night and I wanted to help. My grandmother couldn't safely get down the basement steps to do her own laundry anymore. It was cramped and musty down there as I stood by the sink and scrubbed.

159

By the time I was done, it was almost eleven — time to meet my grandma at the bus stop and walk her home. Before I moved in, she walked home alone on nights when my dad was still at work. But she had told me about the times her purse had been stolen and I knew how unsafe that was, so I headed back out.

There was a completely different vibe out there than there had been early in the morning. Everyone was out — groups of girls and guys hanging out and playing music and kids running around in the street. I felt a little bit safer under the cover of the crowds, but I made sure to add a slight bounce to my walk, a little swagger. After my grandma got off the bus, we slowly walked home together. She held on to my arm and asked me about my day.

When we got home, I finally started on my homework and all the extra reading I was determined to do. Without a computer, I wrote out all my essays and homework by hand. I didn't have a desk, so I sat at the kitchen table, but it was dark in there. There was a problem with the electrical current on the first floor of the house. We had one small table lamp that worked, but it was dim. I was still awake, reading in the faint light, when my dad got home just a couple of hours before my alarm went off again.

Pretty much every day was like this. About a month into the school year, my dad decided that I needed a space of my own where I could work and sleep and have a little privacy. Over the course of a weekend, we cleared out a section of the basement that was just big enough to fit a small desk and a couch for me to sleep on. Then, on Sunday night, Lee told me, "I'll move down to the basement, Zach, and you can have my room."

I was grateful to Lee for this. Now I had a bed to sleep in and a desk. We even got a laptop I could do my homework on. This was a huge improvement. But soon after I moved into the bedroom, there was a big storm, and the hole in the ceiling completely opened up. My bed was directly below the hole, and the room was so small that there was nowhere else to move the bed. I strategically placed several buckets in my room to collect the rainwater. One of them sat at the foot of my bed. Many times I woke up soaking wet because I had accidentally kicked the bucket over in my sleep.

But the hole in my ceiling didn't just let in rain. Squirrels, raccoons, anything that could climb onto the roof, could make its way into my room. Sometimes mice literally fell out of the ceiling. My desk was old and didn't stand up straight, so I propped it up on one side with a few books from my huge and ever-growing collection.

I showed up at school every day exhausted from the efforts it took for me to get there but excited about everything I was learning. Many of the teachers at Bullis were phenomenal educators. They were passionate about their jobs and always willing to put in extra time. I often stayed after school for hours when I didn't have practice, talking to a teacher about a book I'd read, an idea I'd had, or how I could improve my writing. We developed close relationships, and I saw them as role models. Many of them contributed to my intellectual growth and development in ways that I had never experienced before and haven't since.

My favorite teacher freshman year was my history teacher, Mr. Brock. He not only encouraged my questioning in class more than any other teacher but also taught me how to refine my questions. Whenever I asked him about current events before or after class, he would answer my questions thoughtfully and then explain how reframing certain questions could complicate or add nuance to any given answer.

Mr. Brock set the stage for the type of

professor I hoped to find one day at college by teaching history in a way that was utterly captivating. I looked forward to his class; it was intellectually exhilarating. He made us laugh, hopped on top of the table to get our attention, and most of all he knew his stuff and how to get each student to fully engage with the material.

At the beginning of the year, I was having such a hard time with the transition to DC and to Bullis that my grades weren't where I wanted them to be. My first trimester, I got a B+ in history. That wasn't good enough for me. I went to Mr. Brock after school. "I want to get one hundred in your class," I told him. "But it's not just about the grade. I want to be able to use everything I learn in your class later on in life. I want to learn more and for that knowledge to be ingrained."

From then on, Mr. Brock took me under his wing and taught me not just about history but how to be a better student and learner. After school, he taught me studying, note taking, and research techniques, how and why to reread material to gain a deeper understanding of the content. He helped me make the most of my own intelligence and ambition, and it showed in my grades and in my growing base of knowledge.

Mr. Brock pushed me, and I appreciated it. He encouraged all of his students to go above and beyond, and I took advantage of every opportunity I could. After handing in one essay I'd written as an extra assignment, he said, "I know you like to sweat," and I did. By mid-year, I was writing extra papers or giving presentations on historical figures I'd researched almost every week.

Mr. Brock encouraged me to be friends with his son, Hollis, who was in my grade at Bullis. He knew that we had similar intellectual interests and thought we'd be positive influences on each other. Hollis was a top student and a terrific writer, and we quickly became friends. I learned a lot from observing Hollis. He was polished, astute, persistent, and meticulous. If a teacher said it, Hollis had it written down. His notes were gold: neatly organized, stylized, and color coded. His opinions were usually charitable, his answers always canny. No matter the question or conversation, Hollis would tell you precisely what he wanted you to know. Nothing more, nothing less. I'd never met someone that generous, who still managed to jealously guard his time.

I wanted to earn the respect of the top

students at Bullis like Hollis, but it was also important to me to get along with the guys I knew from the football team. Some of them, like one guy named Devon, didn't think that raising your hand in class was cool, so this wasn't always easy.

It was still early in the academic year when I got to school one morning and saw Devon riding in the passenger seat of the Range Rover belonging to a popular white girl named Kelly. The top was down, and rap music was blasting from the stereo. Devon had his feet up on the dashboard, adorned in a pair of Gucci flip-flops that Kelly had given him as a gift the day before.

Devon was something else. He was from the projects and was at Bullis on an athletic scholarship. Because of his background and public school education before arriving at Bullis, his ability to communicate was affected at the most basic level. His speech was slurred and so full of slang that sometimes even I couldn't understand what he was saying.

A lot of students just wrote off Devon as stupid, but talking to him made me recall a number of studies I'd read that demonstrated that verbal fluency and acuity have a lot to do with the amount of words babies and young children are exposed to.

Owing to a lack of opportunity and education, Devon probably wasn't exposed to nearly as many words as I was in my early years. It also made me realize how important it was for parents to read to their kids and encourage them to read. My mom made many mistakes, but when she got me my first library card, she made sure I understood that that card gave me access to a free education, one that could pay great dividends in the future.

Yet some of the white girls at Bullis flocked to Devon. Every couple of weeks, I'd see him walking down the hallway with a different girl on his arm. This was fairly common among some of the black athletes, and I noticed the subtly sour way some teachers looked at them when they saw this.

Intellectually, I was familiar with the history of black men and white women in America — the accusations of rape, the lynching, the myths about predatory black male sexuality, and the stereotypes of black men that hold a fascination for white women and vice versa — but this was the first time I saw it all play out in a brief, slightly displeased expression on a teacher's face. If I'd asked those teachers if they were thinking about that history when they looked at Devon and Kelly, of course they would have said no. And I believe they would have meant it. But I also knew that some things like this were so visceral and yet so taboo that they defied explanation.

As I walked past Devon and Kelly in the Range Rover that day, I wondered whether dating a white girl would complicate the way people at Bullis saw me. I was nothing like Devon, but I was still a young black man at a predominantly white school, and I had no interest in triggering any deep-seated feelings about black bodies that certain teachers or students may have had. It was something I'd have to be mindful of.

Soon after, I attended a freshman-year homecoming dinner at an upscale steak house. Besides me, Devon was the only other black guy at my table. Everyone began their four-course meals with exotic delicacies and hors d'oeuvres. This was normal for most of the other guys: lobster salad on endive spears, Russian caviar with crème fraîche, carrot roulades with radish, fried calamari, and prosciutto and melon. Unlike most of the other kids, I had to look at the menu. After a brief glance, I ordered olive straws and a focaccia cake with spinach dip because they were the only things on the menu that I recognized.

Devon asked the waiter if they had noodles. The waiter asked him what kind. "Like ramen, Cup O' Noodles," he said. Everyone looked at him askance.

"Unfortunately, sir, we don't have ramen," the waiter said. "I'm sorry. Is there anything else you would like?"

"Gimme a burger, with ketchup," Devon replied. After ordering, he sat slumped over in his seat, bobbing his head to rap music that I could overhear from the other side of the table. He had his earphones on the entire time.

When the food came, Devon ate as if someone were going to take his food away if he didn't eat it fast enough. In between bites, he started performing go-go beats on the dinner table while the rest of us were talking. People looked on with disdain.

I was embarrassed, but I felt powerless to intervene. I didn't know Devon well enough then to make eye contact with him or to gesture subtly in some way that suggested he act a little more appropriately. The best I could do while we were there was to direct the group's attention away from him and onto me, so I tried to distract everyone by engaging them in a conversation about what made me decide to come to Bullis.

After that evening, Devon was the butt of many jokes, all made behind his back. No one said anything derisive to his face because he was from a rough neighborhood, much like mine, where looking at someone the wrong way could get you killed. Over the next year, I got to know Devon a little better, and though we were never close, I came to respect his commitment to the sport of football. He probably worked as hard as any athlete I knew at Bullis.

At the next football game, I finally got some playing time. I wanted to compete, to prove to my teammates, my coaches, and myself that I could hit with reckless abandon and make a big play. But I had aggression without technique, and before I knew it, I was injured.

During the second quarter, a player from the other team had the ball and was running toward me. I attempted to tackle him and got an assist from another guy on my team. He got his hands on the ball, and in the tumult my finger got caught inside his helmet. As he drove through the pile, my left hand was fractured in two places, and the bone in my middle finger suffered a clean break. For the next couple of weeks I had a cast covering my entire hand. I was done with football for the season, and I was supposed to go to physical therapy, but I could barely afford one appointment.

Just like that, everything went from challenging to damn near impossible. With a cast on one hand, it took longer to shower and dress myself. It also took twice as long for me to type up assignments, and even my commute now held an extra layer of tension. Some of the guys on the bus knew my face by then. "Aye, yo, you a bitch nigga!" they said when they saw my cast. "You let those niggas stomp you, Moe?"

From time to time, guys on the Metro saw the cast and tried to punk me. Other times, they wanted me to empty my wallet or give up my seat. More often than not, I was more afraid than I would have liked to admit. But every so often, I'm not sure what happened. I would feel so stressed. So frustrated. So tense and fed up that I'd almost stop caring. On those days, I was just waiting for someone to fuck with me, because I'd rather die than allow my circumstances to shatter my resolve.

Another thing that happened frequently on the bus that was always hard for me to watch was when black parents hit their kids. I had read the research on how violence begets violence. The history of unrestrained brutality against black people from the time of slavery through Jim Crow up to today has led to a cultural pattern of violence in black communities and even within families. I felt deeply for these parents, who had probably experienced the same thing in their own childhoods. I understood that, by hitting me, even my own mother was just repeating what her father had done to her. But that didn't make it any easier for me to experience this or witness it, and I knew it was possible to break this cycle because my dad, who had been beaten by his grandfather, never once hit me.

One night after seeing a particularly disturbing scene on the bus between a mother and her child, I asked my dad about this. "Why do you think your grandfather got mad so easily?" I asked him.

My dad blew out a big breath and rubbed the smooth top of his head as he looked at the ground. "That was just part of the times back then," he said.

"A lot of scholars write about how violence leads to more violence, and how kids who are hit build up anger and resentment that makes them more confrontational," I told him. My dad wasn't one to read scholarly journals, but he understood a lot of things intuitively. He observed the world around him but didn't often say much out loud about all the things he'd noticed. "You never hit me and Nicole," I continued. "But most dads in this neighborhood whup their kids. Do you think that's because of your grandfather?"

My dad just shook his head and looked off in the distance. "I don't know," he finally said. "I just never wanted to do that with my kids."

Without football taking up my time, I threw myself deeper into my academic and social life at Bullis. I joined Model UN and started tutoring other students after school. No matter how much of my own work I had to do, I always made time to help other people. I liked how it felt to be known as someone other people could count on. About halfway through the year, I realized that I would be able to help more people if I tutored younger students in other subjects, so I signed up to tutor students between grades six and nine in any subject they needed help with.

I poured myself into every interaction, channeling all my anxiety and frustration into being present and dependable and having more bandwidth than many would imagine possible. Part of this was a healthy distraction. I wasn't afraid of home anymore the way I had been with my mom, but I still didn't look forward to being there. It wasn't a relaxing or enriching environment. School was the only place where I could not only better myself but also work to better others. That was rewarding.

Ultimately, I liked the look on my teacher's face when I handed in an extra essay I'd written based on a simple comment he or she had made. It made me feel good about myself, like I was more than just a kid from a rough part of DC with a mentally ill mom and a hole over his head who showered in a soiled, rotting bathroom every day.

Most of my friendships at Bullis started with my demonstrating intelligence in conversation or helping another student with a paper or assignment. Even with the top students in the grade, I wasn't satisfied unless I could teach them something; until they saw me the same way the rest of the kids at Bullis saw them. One kid named Todd was possibly the smartest and definitely the most competitive student in my grade. He was a math genius and a bit of an intellectual bully who intimidated some of the other kids at Bullis.

The first few times I spoke to Todd I could tell he was evaluating me by asking me a series of questions: "What do your parents do?" "Where did you go to school before this?" He even challenged me to solve some complicated math problems that I hardly understood, just to prove his dominance. Then he pulled up a video from *Saturday Night Live* on his phone that showed black people acting "irate and out of control" and said, "I know you know what this is like."

Todd brought out my competitive instincts in a way that no other student had. He had every advantage; his family was wealthy, and he lived eight minutes from the school. And yet he assumed that anyone who didn't achieve as much as he did was simply inferior. Freshman year, he petitioned the principal to have the scholarship kids who had been brought to Bullis to play sports (most of whom were black) kicked out of the school, claiming that they were "a different kind of stupid."

When I visited his house, I began to understand where these attitudes came from. I saw the conditions under which he did his work, and they couldn't have been more different from mine. On the side of Todd's house, there was a lavish solarium where he liked to hang out, with a sloped roof, hardwood floors, and half a dozen comfortable chaise lounges. During the day, the room was filled with sunlight. And as soon as the sun went down, recessed lights automatically turned on, bouncing luminous rays off the ceiling's glass panes. Every time I was in there, I thought about the electrical problems in my grandmother's house and how hard it was to find a spot with enough light to read by.

Todd had every possible convenience and even luxury at his fingertips, and I saw that his vision of meritocracy and personal responsibility came precisely from his own privileged lifestyle. He'd never experienced obstacles or hardships. His experiences taught him that being smart and working hard got him everything he wanted, so he believed that anyone in a bad position was there because of innate character flaws rather than circumstances.

I realized then that privilege breeds that sort of demeanor, an aura that is immune to changing circumstances. Todd had never felt the pressure I did every single day to adapt or pretend. Throughout his life, he would rarely, if ever, have to revise the parameters of his comportment to appeal to people, and when he did, he could afford to barely change his behavior.

What I wanted to say to Todd was, "Talk to me about personal responsibility when you face disadvantage after disadvantage," but I took a different tack. The other thing I'd learned from being at his house was that his political beliefs came straight from his dad. Around the dinner table, his parents talked about what a shame it was that they were sending him to a private school where there were so many "inferior" athletic scholarship students. Todd hadn't studied these issues the way I had. He saw them only from his own perspective, which had been entirely informed by his dad's opinions. When I discovered these intellectual weaknesses, I didn't hesitate to take advantage of them, using Todd's own tricks against him.

"I see that you have some strong opinions about race," I told him after dinner as we hung out in the solarium. "But you seem oblivious to some historical facts." Going from one source to another, I forced Todd to admit to the holes in his knowledge. "Do you agree that there is a relationship between race and wealth?" I asked him. When he said yes, I asked, "So what studies are you familiar with on the intersection of race and economics? What research informs your opinion?" Then I broke down the information in the texts he'd never read, forcing him to see that he couldn't compete because he hadn't read the relevant literature.

It took time, but eventually, this technique worked. Todd was so competitive that he couldn't accept the fact that there were things I knew more about than he did, so he started to let me teach him. We spent hours talking about politics, race, economics, and affirmative action. I got him to read the work of Cornel West and other scholars I admired, and little by little Todd's beliefs actually began to change. The next time I was at his house for dinner, Todd brought up Cornel West and his dad's response was, "What is he, just another black professor who studies race?"

"No, Dad," Todd said angrily. "He actually has a lot of interesting things to say." As Todd and his dad continued arguing around their custom-made triangular kitchen table, I couldn't help but smile to myself. There were so many days when I was sick of working so hard and doing all these mental gymnastics just to differentiate myself. I was angry and frustrated all the time about the ways that my life was so much harder than my peers' just because of the situation I was born into. And on top of that, I had to achieve more than they did just to be seen as an equal. I had to possess knowledge that went beyond what we studied for a history test. I had to read more than my classmates and prove that my mind was of value, because I understood that my mind was what had gotten me into Bullis in the first place.

This pressure was almost unbearable at times. Yet I knew that if I wanted to attend a top college and be successful, these were the same pressures I'd be facing throughout my life. Would it have been nice to go to school with people who were more culturally aware and sensitive? Sure, it would have spared my feelings. But if my life had taught me anything by then, it was that the world was not concerned with my feelings. I couldn't hide from racism or insensitivity; I had to learn how to deal with it. The truth is that there was no place I could have gone where race would not have been an issue for me. Hiding from race is not an option for black people in this country. So I had no choice but to confront it head-on by doing everything I could to represent all the things that most people assumed black people couldn't do.

My success with someone like Todd gave me hope that if I kept pushing forward, I could actually create positive change, even on an individual level. It motivated me to keep going even during the most difficult times.

At the end of the school year, each department handed out an award for the best student in that subject, and Mr. Brock selected me to receive the history award. It was a huge honor that I knew would go a long way in setting me apart. Hollis and I also won the election to be co–class presidents for the following year. I finally felt like I was zoned in, focused, and back at the top of my game after the difficult move and transition to DC, yet I remained ever vigilant, not knowing what obstacles were waiting for me around each corner.

CHAPTER 6
THE VOID

I started my sophomore year at Bullis fired up to do and learn as much as possible. I ran track and was co–class president; served as a student tutor and a student tutor supervisor; was a student ambassador, a peer mentor, and secretary of Model UN; and began attending student leadership conferences every trimester. I was rarely at home. After school, I tutored for as long as I could, helping students with homework, studying, papers, or whatever they needed. Then I stayed and did my own work in the library until it closed. On the weekends, I spent most of my time at my friends' houses.

That year I also formed a new friendship. Like me, Drew was one of the few black kids at Bullis who were taken seriously and seen as smart and ambitious, even though Bullis recruited him to play football. Unlike me, Drew's dad was pretty well-off. His parents were separated, and I hung out with

Drew at his mom's house all the time. She had him make a list of goals for every month, and pretty soon Drew told me that he was basing some of those lists on goals I'd told Drew I was trying to accomplish myself.

Despite our different backgrounds, Drew understood some things about me that someone like Hollis or James, another friend of mine, could never fully understand. If another student made a racially insensitive joke in class or a disparaging comment about Obama, Drew and I would catch each other's eye. Sometimes if we saw some of the other black students playing to a stereotype, we looked at each other and knew exactly what we were both thinking.

Drew, Hollis, Todd, and James were some of the top students in my grade. They didn't need my help. Yet when I was at their homes I still felt compelled to prove my value. If they had younger siblings, sometimes I helped them with their homework or essays. With the others, I had in-depth intellectual conversations, made frequent book recommendations, or explained aspects of political and economic policy that they were curious about. Basically, I showcased my knowledge, and this enabled me to capture their interest and demonstrate my value to them and their families.

But sometimes when we hung out, my friends just wanted to relax and have fun. I could do this with Drew a bit more than the others, but even with him, I would usually stay up late reading after he went to sleep. For me, taking it easy was hardly an option. I never forgot what Papa had told me all those years before — the pressures were different for me. James was my Model UN partner. He was naturally very smart and a great intellectual partner in crime. We balanced each other well and at the conferences we attended together, we killed it. The weekend before a conference early in the year, I slept over at his house so that we could work on our opening statement and summation speech together.

At 8:30 a.m., I woke up, ready to get started. I left the guest room where I slept and walked down the long, wood-paneled hallway to James's room. He was asleep, but when he heard me come in, James rolled over, looked at me in disbelief, asked, "What are you doing?" and went back to sleep. I sat down at the L-shaped executive desk in the corner of his room and started working, thinking he'd get up soon and join me, but he didn't wake up until 10:00. By then I was almost done with a draft of the speech.

"Let's go get something to eat," he said when I showed him the draft.

James's dad took us to a local bagel shop. The family owned many homes. Their main residence, where we'd stayed the night before, was in Potomac. We sat at an outdoor table in the Potomac Village courtyard, eating our bagels and talking about current events. It was designed to look like a small town or a European village. Bakeries and overpriced markets dotted the square, which was full of local residents enjoying their weekends. Despite the crowds, it was quiet, peaceful.

During conversations like these, I was always interested to learn more about my friends' parents and how they saw the world. I tried to remember the minor, seemingly insignificant details people told me and make sure to bring them up the next time I saw them. This tactic was something my mom had taught me. But for her, creating a sense of loyalty was a way of manipulating people, of endearing them to her so that she could use it later to get what she wanted. I drew a fine line between taking the sparks of brilliance in her methods and the way she twisted loyalty to serve her purposes. For me, it was about building rapport and developing a deeper connection

183

with people. If I understood what mattered to them and, more important, why, I was able to more fully engage.

James's dad had a wealth of knowledge, and we had great conversations about a variety of topics. He was also a pretty conservative guy, so I was always curious to get his take on electoral politics and the strengths and weaknesses of Romney's presidential campaign. Other times, we talked about our favorite books and fascinating social scientific theories we'd read about. With other parents and teachers, I discussed everything from climate change to what they did for a living and how they managed their family businesses. While I wanted these families to know that I was smart and well informed, I also wanted to gain as much knowledge and wisdom from them as I could. So I was often just as eager to listen as I was to talk.

I didn't have the money to pay for newspaper subscriptions, but I had ways of accessing what I needed. I often got to school early and picked up a teacher's discarded copy of the newspaper, and I figured out how to read as much free content as possible by strategically viewing the maximum number of articles on each device before hitting the pay wall. Comments like the one from Todd's dad, writing off Cornel West as "just another black professor who studies race," were always at the back of my mind. So while I was passionate about issues of race, and debated them, I made sure to be armed with plenty of other artillery.

When we finally got back to the house it was noon. We headed upstairs to James's room. "Want to work for a bit?" I asked him.

"Ah, we can work later tonight; it's Saturday," he replied. "Let's just hang for a while." He sat on the leather couch on one side of his room and started playing a video game.

I wasn't mad at James. Why would he want to do so much extra work when just being smart and putting in a modicum of effort had always been enough for him? But that wasn't enough for me. I couldn't let up for one minute and allow him or anyone else to think that I was lazy or content just sitting on my ass and being good when I could be great instead. When friends waved away my desire to keep pushing further and told me to just relax and have fun, I remembered that I would have never gotten into Bullis if it hadn't been for my extreme work ethic and what some called my perfectionism. Without those things, I wouldn't have been there at James's house, either. He certainly wasn't inviting any other kids from my

185

neighborhood to sleep over.

Ultimately, I realized that my insistence on overpreparing was the reason people like James and his family took an interest in me in the first place. I wasn't a family member or a part of their community. So I worked as hard as I could to avoid the feeling of missed opportunity, which is really just another way of saying that I overprepared when I couldn't prove that my life had been about more than pain and my efforts to overcome it.

As James played, I went downstairs to the kitchen, where his thirteen-year-old sister, Anna, was sitting at the large island in the center of the room, working on some history homework. "Do you need any help?" I asked her.

She nodded shyly. "Yeah, I don't understand the Cold War," she said. I hopped onto the high-backed barstool next to her and started working with Anna, patiently explaining how the Cold War didn't involve military combat. After a little while, their mom came in and saw me helping her.

"Oh, Zach, you're such a nice young man," she told me with a warm smile. "Would you like something to eat? How about a grilled cheese sandwich?" I nodded, and she walked over to the double range and quickly made the sandwich, cutting it in half on the diagonal before bringing it over to me.

"Thank you," I said.

"No, thank *you*, Zach," she told me, putting a hand on my shoulder. Then as she walked away, she said, "If you keep helping Anna with her homework, I'll bring you another sandwich." I was happy to help. It felt good to be able to. But the idea of being rewarded with food was off-putting. Despite her mom's comment, I continued helping Anna anyway.

My visits to friends' houses were often problematic in one way or another. The next time I was at James's house for dinner, I told his family about my commute. My intention was just to explain to them how difficult and long a trip it was, and how mad and confrontational some of the people I encountered were. But they were fascinated, and they wanted more.

"Zach, do an impersonation of a thug," James told me as we sat in his family's formal dining room. The burgundy chairs accentuated the natural red tones in the rich wood that flanked the room, from the wide columns that divided it from the adjoining living room to the sixteen-seat table. "Come on, man, do it."

187

I hesitated. I had seen other black kids in situations like this so many times, and I always hated it when they capitulated and acted like a clown. I'd managed to avoid doing it myself by strategically shifting the conversation in one direction or another. But this time, all eyes were on me, demanding a performance.

The brave thing to do would have been to say, "No, I don't feel comfortable doing that," and to explain why. But as I sat there at their table eating their food, I wondered how warmly I would be welcomed back next time if I said no. As complicated as some of my friendships could be at times, I needed them. I didn't have a family that sat around the table together like this — our small kitchen table didn't even fit all five of us around it — or even a comfortable place at home to read or do my work. I gained a lot from these friendships and felt obligated to give and give and give in return.

So, for a moment, I did it. I assumed an entirely different demeanor and talked to them like a guy I had seen on the bus that morning. I impersonated his slang, his slur, and his aggressive inflection. James and his family roared with laughter and begged me to do it again and again.

On the long bus ride home later, I tried to

tell myself that it wasn't a big deal. Black comedians did stuff like that all the time, and there was value in humor. Plenty of my friends made jokes about race, and I often laughed at those jokes and made my own. Why? Because I found them funny. But in this case, I knew I hadn't lived up to my own ideal. In my own way, I had contributed to perpetuating stereotypes of black people — the one thing I worked tirelessly, gave up sleep, and went out of my way to avoid doing.

The next time I was at James's house they begged me to do the impersonation again. This time I was prepared. Instead of hesitating or showing how much this bothered me, I responded with a warm smile and a quick shift in the conversation to the Model UN conference we had coming up. Once again, I thought of my mom. She had always told me that showing too much emotion, like indecision, gave smart people power over you, so it was important to know how to keep it cool. The dispassionate response, she said, was always even-keeled, never too high, never too low, almost cold-blooded, but with a smile warm enough to lend the impression of goodwill.

My mom was almost always right about these things, and changing the subject worked, mostly. But I sensed the energy in the room shift along with the conversation. James and his family were miffed and caught off guard, unused to not getting their way. Suddenly, they seemed a little less enthusiastic about having me there, slightly less effusive than usual when praising my explanation of whatever issue we were discussing.

After dinner I spent an hour helping Anna with her English essay. I had my own ways of avoiding their displeasure without demeaning myself.

In school, my academic focus was mostly on writing. That year, the author Reginald Dwayne Betts came to Bullis as a writer in residence. Dwayne had just published his memoir, *A Question of Freedom,* about spending eight years in prison after his first offense, committed at age sixteen. In prison, Dwayne graduated from high school and began reading and writing poetry.

Dwayne's visit was truly inspiring. His message was at once challenging and uplifting, universal and yet unique. What struck me most was the lack of shame he seemed to carry about his past. I wanted to follow his example, to unabashedly own the fact that my experiences had indeed informed some of my strongest beliefs and opinions. The freedom, confidence, and authenticity with which he shared his message were things I aspired to. Most of all, meeting him compelled me to imagine what it would mean for me to tell my story one day.

My English teacher that year, Ms. Heninger, was a disarmingly genuine, brilliant educator who helped me improve my writing probably more than anyone else. I spent hours with her in the classroom after school, going through my essays sentence by sentence and analyzing the impact of every word choice. "Let's find le bon mot," she told me — the right word. She took what I said and made it stronger by framing it slightly differently, a technique that allowed me to refine my own arguments by improving the clarity of my writing.

But perhaps the best thing Ms. Heninger did for me was recommend that I share some of my poems with another English teacher, Ms. Chehak, who ran Bullis's National Poetry Month activities. Ms. Chehak read all my poems and gave me extensive feedback on each of them. Then she encouraged me to read my work at the Jazz Café, a nighttime event held twice a year when students performed at Bullis's Blair Family Center for the Arts, a vast building on campus that held studio spaces for visual and performing arts students and a state-of-the-art 750-seat theater.

We selected a poem I had written that I called "A Bluesman in the Life of the Mind, a Jazzman in the World of Ideas," which was a line Cornel West used to describe himself in his memoir. It was a poem about spiritual and literal poverty, a call for moral courage and a stronger fiber of resilience. The content was good, but on the night of the performance I was entirely focused on my delivery.

I didn't want just to recite the poem well; I wanted parents in the audience who didn't know me to ask the person beside them who I was. I wanted my performance to resonate, affirm, and illuminate my determination to matter more, to be of greater value in the hearts and minds of every person I had ever made eye contact with. When I heard the applause echo throughout the proscenium theater and saw the expressions on the audience members' faces when I was done, I knew I had achieved my goal.

Another goal I had during sophomore year was to broaden my knowledge of literature and philosophy beyond the Western canon. One teacher who had a big impact on me that year was my history teacher, Dr. Sun.

He introduced me to Chinese moral philosophy and the whole idea of comparative philosophy — that our culture greatly determines what we view as right or wrong. This challenged me to acknowledge that I viewed my own principles through a lens of Western moral values and made me wonder if there was such a thing as a universal right and wrong.

Dr. Sun and I also spent a lot of time discussing the differences between activism and intellectualism. I had a passion for social justice and was beginning to question what I felt called to do with my life. For a long time, I had felt a call to public service, to ask the most difficult questions and find answers that would help address those questions. Dr. Sun explained that intellectuals must prioritize evidence when looking at solutions, while activists push for radical change, sometimes pushing politicians to do more than they otherwise would. He made me think that with my natural hunger for learning and probing, the world of academia and politics was ultimately where I belonged.

Like Dr. Sun and many of my teachers, Ms. Chehak gave me book recommendations and often sent me home with a stack of books to read. Ms. Chehak knew African

193

American history extremely well and recommended books by black feminist scholars such as bell hooks and Hortense Spillers that stretched and complicated my own thoughts and beliefs about race.

Reading these works, I saw how frequently black women had been left out of the picture, while scholars, often black men, discussed issues of race and class. Many black intellectuals spoke about the experience of racism mainly, and sometimes exclusively, from a black male perspective, highlighting the various ways their humanity had been degraded and denied. While this discussion was something I cared about deeply, it was rarely balanced with one about all the unique ways in which black women have suffered. Even the scholars who spoke about race without focusing so much on the particular experience of black men still failed to fully capture and dissect the compounded challenges black women faced as they dealt with racism and sexism.

The result of discussions of race being unfairly tilted toward the male point of view is that the experiences of black women have taken a backseat to those of black men, although they've suffered in ways that black men haven't. Racism and sexism were stacked against them. And too often they've borne the brunt of the very masculinity that has been historically debased in black men when black men asserted their power over the only people they could — black women.

Once I started reading about this, I couldn't stop. I tore through book after book, and then went back to the works of some of the black intellectuals I admired most to see if I'd missed anything they'd said. There were some heartening exceptions, such as W. E. B. DuBois, who devoted an entire chapter of his book *Darkwater* to the experience of black women in America — not only their suffering but also their agency, resistance, and strength. Still, I was disappointed to find that even some of the most admirable figures in our history, such as Martin Luther King Jr., did not attend to the unique struggles of black women. In the history of civil rights, men have largely dominated the story line and taken up space instead of leaving equal room beside them for black women.

The hard truth is that black men have contributed to these struggles both subtly and overtly. When black men talk about being stepped on by the world or all the ways in which their opportunities have been constrained and their humanity devalued, they rarely follow with, "and black women

195

have it even worse than we do." More obviously, we contribute to the degradation of black women by glorifying the kind of common rap that reduces them to bitches, hos, and body parts. As a result of all the things we say or don't say, we are complicit.

This forced me to look again at the women in my family and see their experiences in a new light. Years before, Lola had told me that there was a time when she wanted to become a school principal, but there was a black man at her school who had discouraged her. Now I saw that this was likely because of competition within the race and black men's tendency to put themselves first in a patriarchal society. If there was room at the top for one black person, it was going to be a black man, not a woman. This dates back to the fight for black suffrage, when leaders such as Frederick Douglass supported black women's suffrage but for various reasons put black men's suffrage first.

My grandma Pearl had also suffered at the hands of black men. Her husband was abusive and did little to help raise their three kids. She was a working-class black woman with few opportunities, but she almost never talked about the things she'd lived through. It was as if she'd been led to believe that the pain of her experiences was not worth discussing.

I realized that reading these books by black feminist scholars also provided a new lens through which to see my own mother. Was it possible that my mom looked at me and saw all the black men who had hurt her or put their own pain above her own? Was that why she so badly wanted to control me?

Once again, I saw my dad trying to break this pattern. In the middle of my sophomore year, he got a car. Whenever he had a car, it was usually so old and beat-up that it didn't last long, but while it was still running he drove us down to Lynchburg, Virginia, to visit my grandma's brother Ray and his wife, Annette. When we got in the car, my dad made a point of opening the door for Nicole and my grandmother. Nicole was getting older and starting to get embarrassed by things like this. "Dad, stop it," she said as he held the door open.

My dad shook his head. "I want you to know what you should expect when you start dating one day," he told her.

As we made the long drive to Virginia, we listened to the radio. A Drake song came on, and Nicole started singing along. "Stop it," my dad said, reaching over to turn off the radio. "Think about what you're singing. That song is degrading women."

At Ray and Annette's house, I got to see a type of relationship between a black man and a black woman that was different from most of the ones I'd been exposed to. Ray and Annette had played an active role in helping to raise my dad when he was living with his grandmother. They also raised four kids of their own. They are an example of a black family functioning the way it should. Ray and Annette have an equal balance of power. They shared the responsibilities of raising their kids, and that night, Annette cooked dinner and then Ray cleaned all the dishes. They were a team, and I saw that black families could be stronger if they stood together, working and fighting and loving and resisting side by side.

We were about halfway home that night when we heard a horrible hissing sound coming from the car. Smoke started billowing from the hood. I was in the backseat with Nicole, and our grandmother was asleep in the passenger seat. "Um, Dad," I said, "I think there's something wrong with the car."

I was only trying to help, but it was clearly the worst thing I could have said. In response, my dad just turned around and looked at me. I could barely return his gaze. There was so much pain in his eyes. All the years of hard work, of worry and struggle, of taking one step forward and two steps back, of always trying to do the right thing just to get knocked back down again — it was all there in his eyes.

Without saying a word, my dad pulled the car over to the side of the road, leaned forward, and put his head in his hands. It was a desolate place with nothing but more road as far as I could see. My dad got out and tried tinkering under the hood. I got in the driver's seat and tried to restart the car when he gave the signal, but it kept stalling.

Eventually we called Ray, and he came to pick us up. We had no way of getting home, so he brought us back to their house in Virginia. My dad didn't have enough money for a rental car. A cab ride would cost even more.

"Dad, I have some money I can give you," I said. I was saving the money I had earned from writing competitions and odd jobs I did for Mrs. Brown and some other seniors in the neighborhood. Sitting in Ray and Annette's modest living room, my dad shook his head. I knew how badly he didn't want to take money from me. But what choice did he have? "Are you sure?" I asked him.

My dad shook his head again, but this

time he said, "Yeah, I may have to borrow a little bit."

After we got home, I used the rest of that money to buy tickets for my dad and me to attend a lecture by Cornel West, who was going to be speaking in DC soon after. This was a chance to meet one of my heroes, and I was excited. I had already read almost all of West's work, but I made it my mission to reread all twenty-two of his books before the lecture, which was only a couple of weeks away. It wasn't enough for me just to attend the lecture. I needed to be able to stand out, to say something clear-sighted and discerning to West about his work to make an impression that would prove I mattered.

To get all this done, I cut sleep down to the bare minimum, maybe three hours a night. But after five days, I'd gotten through only five books. At this rate, I wouldn't finish in time. So I gave up sleep entirely and skipped most meals. I got home from school at around nine o'clock, did my homework, and then started reading until it was time to leave for school in the morning. I got through the books more quickly this way, but I was hurting. It was hard to stay awake in class, and I wanted to be as alert and focused as ever.

I asked my dad to get me a case of Red Bull so it would be easier to stay awake, but he refused. I begged, and he finally relented, but he brought home only a few cans instead of a full case. He probably thought I'd drink one a night over the next few nights, but instead I drank them all right then and there, sat down at my wobbly desk, and got back to reading.

After a few minutes, I started to feel weird. Beads of sweat pricked my skin, and my vision became a little hazy. The words on the page didn't appear as crisp as usual. But I'd been going without much sleep for so long that I knew how to push through those feelings, zone in, and focus. After a few more minutes, the words on the page were swimming and the room started to spin around me. I tried to grab onto the side of my desk for balance, but I collapsed. As I fell from my chair, I hit my head on the corner of my desk. I could feel my body convulsing as I crawled toward my bed and somehow managed to get on top of it, with one leg hanging off the side.

My dad heard me fall but thought I had just dropped something and sent Nicole to check on me. She came into the room and found me sprawled on the bed, unresponsive, with my eyes drooping off to the side.

"Dad!" she screamed. "What happened to Zach?" My dad ran into the room. When he saw me lying there, he bent down and started shaking me. I was awake, and I could see and hear everything that was going on, but I couldn't move. It seemed like some form of sleep paralysis or maybe what it would feel like to be in a coma with my eyes open.

"Zach!" my dad yelled, shaking me. "Zach!" Then I heard him mutter, "Shit." In the background, Nicole was panicking, asking if she should call 911. I wanted to console her and say that everything was going to be fine, but I felt paralyzed. My dad ran out of the room and came back with a cup of water. He handed it to me, and it fell out of my hand. He left the room again to refill it, and when he came back, he tried to prop me up with one arm and pour the water into my mouth with the other. The liquid ran down the side of my face and onto the bed. "Shit," my dad muttered again, and then picked me up and threw me over his shoulder.

Outside, my dad laid me down on the backseat of the car and drove me to the hospital. By the time we got there, I was somewhat more lucid, but everything was still blurred, and I was slurring my words.

When they asked me my name, I was so discombobulated that I gave them my middle name, Royce.

I thought the doctors were just going to tell me to get more sleep and send me on my way, but instead they admitted me, and I realized I was going to be there for a while. I turned to my dad from the hospital bed. I was attached to an IV drip and had tubes to monitor my blood pressure and oxygen levels coming out of my nose. "Can you go home and bring me back those books?" I asked him.

My dad looked at me with a potent mix of concern and fury. I don't think I'd ever seen him so mad. But even then, his words were spare. "No, Zach," was all he said.

I was in the hospital for two days with a case of extreme exhaustion and dehydration. Drinking all that caffeine on an empty stomach had compounded everything. Since I had started at Bullis, I hadn't missed a single day of school, and when I checked my phone, I had several texts from friends, asking where I was and whether I could still help them study or do their homework. I hated the way it felt to disappoint them. Ever since I was a little boy, reading about Martin Luther King in Lola and Papa's basement, I'd done everything I could to be someone whom people could count on. When I said I was going to do something, I did it, and I resented being put on my back by something as pointless as sleep.

On the way home from the hospital, my dad tried to talk to me some more. "You need to eat. You need to sleep. You need some balance, Zach," he told me. "You need to start taking care of yourself." It was my turn to be quiet. I knew intellectually that he was right. Of course he was. But I also knew that I wasn't going to listen to him. There was too much at stake for me to loosen my grip on the reins now.

I went back to school the next day. On my way home, I was tired. It felt as if I were recovering from a bad flu. I still had a stack of books to get through, and I knew I wouldn't be able to stay awake for long. But I knew better than to ask my dad for help this time. So I stopped at a deli on the way home to pick up some more Red Bull.

While I was waiting in line at the deli I texted back and forth with Drew. I told him that I was getting some more Red Bull so that I could stay up that night and finish reading. "You're crazy; don't do that," he wrote. At first I laughed it off, but then he got serious. "Why do you feel like you have to read all those books?"

I stopped and thought about it for a minute. I had an easy answer ready, the one I told other people and myself — that I wanted to be prepared for any scenario and make the best possible impression. But why were those things so important to me? Why did I have to perform not just well but superbly, be not just one of the smartest students but the most knowledgeable? When would I ever be satisfied? It wasn't as simple as being black and poor and needing to prove myself. After all, I didn't see Devon putting himself in the hospital because he felt he had to read so many books and help as many other students as he could.

I put the Red Bull back in the refrigerated case and got on the bus. I saw Drew's question almost as a riddle that I needed to solve. Papa had always told me that self-knowledge was the most valuable thing a man could possess. So I was determined to fully understand my own impulses.

I started simply thinking about the books I was reading. What did I get from books? Knowledge. Then I asked myself why knowledge was so important to me. Why did it feel like something I could never have enough of? I realized that knowledge was one thing that people almost universally valued and respected, even admired. By filling myself with knowledge, I was literally trying to make myself more valuable, more worthy of their respect and admiration.

The hardest question to face but the easiest to answer was why I didn't already feel valuable. When the one person who was supposed to love me unconditionally told me over and over that I was a worthless, ungrateful punk, it became hard to ever truly believe that I was good enough. Some of my earliest memories are of my mom saying things that made me feel unworthy of ever being liked or loved. And now I was trying to fill the void this left inside me with knowledge, and therefore value.

Over the years I'd told myself that if I could talk to enough people and make the ideal impression enough times, they would like me. My credentials and skills, and ultimately my knowledge, would make me worth liking. And if enough people liked me, I would matter. I'd be worth something. But, I realized on that long bus ride home, no matter how much I knew or read or learned, those memories would always be a part of me.

The only answer was to keep drawing that fine line between the good and the evil, just like the moral philosophers Dr. Sun had taught me about. There was no universal right and wrong. My mom was like a weight around my neck, but at the same time so much of her advice had buoyed me. All I could do was try to tease apart that distinction, use the good pieces that I pried from the bad to help others, and leave the rest behind.

CHAPTER 7
GRAVITY

I could feel the beat thumping in my rib cage as I walked past the subwoofer. It was simple but hypnotic. Every head bobbed as 50 Cent's "In Da Club" emanated from the surround sound. Neon strobe lights flashed across the hardwood floor. Pockets of haze dispersed throughout the room. The crowds were loosely packed, some dancing, others talking. The theme was "school's out"; the venue, a party for high school students in the area, reserved at a local night club in Bethesda. I'd decided to go with Drew after he told me about it.

To this point, I'd been to some middle school dances, a bar mitzvah party, and a homecoming, but this was my first time going out in high school. Drew was talking to a few other guys from Bullis who were there. They were on the football team. But this girl kept glancing at me from across the room, so I was thinking more about how to approach her than what they were saying.

She had long blond hair with subtle features and a slender figure. She was wearing a white crop top with ripped high-waist denim shorts and tan ankle boots. Her makeup was vibrant — bright red lipstick with lilac eyeliner and silver eye shadow, and her cheekbones pronounced with blush. The tonic warmth of her smile was undiminished by the elaborate highlighting. She was glamorous, though I'm not sure if that's what sparked my interest. We'd been making eye contact off and on for only a few minutes, but I'd spotted her earlier that night. It was as if I could feel her presence from across the room, the way she gestured delicately, gracefully extending her hands, as if to pull me in closer; the soft layers of her hair swaying gently over bare shoulders as she laughed. She was already talking to a handful of people, but I wasn't leaving without at least trying to talk to her.

I convinced myself that I had nothing to lose. So I walked over to her and introduced myself. As we started talking, she turned toward me and took a small step forward, deftly distancing herself from her friends, enough for us to have our own conversation. We talked for a few minutes about our summer plans; hers were far more extravagant than mine. Before I knew it, we were dancing. I was leaning on a pillar in the middle of the dance floor when she turned around to kiss me. We'd been making out for only about a minute when the football guys from Bullis whom Drew had been talking to earlier started making a scene.

"Aye, son, she got them dukes, though! I see you, Zach, out here flexing," said Devon, who was the ringleader. "My man Zach got him a snow bunny! Aye, he about to pipe her, yo! My man Zach, about to lay pipe! Blow her back out, Moe! Look at him, son! Aye, y'all," he said to the people standing nearby, "check out my mans over here!"

"Okay, Zach! Slim said he about to beat it up," said Anton, another guy who was rolling with Devon that night.

To my surprise, she didn't seem bothered in the slightest by what they were saying. In fact, all the hype surrounding us made her show off a little bit as we grinded. I tried not to show it, but I felt kind of awkward and a little embarrassed being the center of the spectacle they'd created. They were jumping around, spazzing, and holding on to one another like they were watching the final round of the NBA Slam Dunk Contest. All of the siccin' lasted for maybe two minutes, but of course it felt like a lot longer. I played it off, feigning a mix of slight amusement and subtle approval. But they were being OC (out of control). Had Drew been there at the time, he would have coolly dissuaded them from putting me on blast like that.

Drew was cool, but never too cool to do the right thing. He was a polite, responsible, likable guy who always worked hard and did well at everything he endeavored to do. And I was glad we went out together that night because I knew he had no interest in drinking or smoking or doing anything stupid that would land us both in trouble. After the group of football guys had moved on, I decided to ask the girl for her number. For this to be my first time going out, I thought things were going pretty well.

She pulled out her phone and replied, "How about you give me your number, instead?" As I put my number in her phone, she asked me what sport I played.

"I run track, but only because my school requires you to play a sport," I said.

"Wait, so you're not a football player? Are you on the basketball team?"

"Nah, our team is pretty good. I tried out freshman year, though."

She looked disappointed, like she'd gotten her hopes up for nothing. "Wait, my friend

211

told me that all the guys you were with earlier played for Bullis. You guys won the IAC championship last year, right?"

"Ha, yeah, most of those guys are on the team. I'm just friends with them."

"Okay, well, it was nice meeting you. I'm going to go find my friends. Enjoy the rest of your night." She turned around and walked away before I'd even gotten a chance to say, "It was nice meeting you, too."

To say the least, it was a bit of a letdown. But it felt like even more of a disappointment when I saw her minutes later, making out with a football player from our rival high school. I'd competed against the guy at a couple of track meets. He was yoked, with long dreads and a few tattoos, and seemed to fit more of the "black athlete" mold she was looking for. He was chilling, cupping her ass in his palms as she ran her hands under his shirt.

I posted up on the wall for a bit and watched unobtrusively as they got high together. A few minutes later, Drew came over to tell me that his mom was there to pick us up. On the car ride home, I talked to them about some of my plans for the summer. But later that night, before going to bed, I felt sad.

I thought about everything my mom

would have said about the girl I'd danced with, why she left me for that other guy, and where I was lacking. I thought about what she used to say about Emmett Till, and how I might have ended up if that night had taken place fifty years earlier. I thought about how much appearances mattered, and how being black and poor made them matter even more. I thought about the times I'd lied and said to various friends' parents that I lived near Georgetown or some part of DC that didn't conjure up images of violence and poverty. I thought about how even though Drew was black, he'd never been exposed to the symptoms of poverty and mental illness that often get characterized as black pathology.

Some part of me wanted to see the world through Drew's eyes that night, to experience and live in it the way he did. To be able to look forward to seeing my mom and spending time with her. To be able to feel about my mother the way Drew felt about his.

Since arriving at Bullis, I hadn't really dated. I didn't go to house parties, drink, or smoke weed, though I was invited to do all those things. For one thing, I didn't live in Potomac. Most parties ended after midnight, and the bus lines in Montgomery

County stopped running after 11:00 p.m. So even if I wanted to go to a party at someone's house, it was hardly feasible. I was also very focused — busy working, reading, tutoring, and applying for various leadership conferences and academic summer programs. But there was another factor: I was intensely cognizant of how every move I made could be perceived. It had taken years, but I'd established myself as a model student, a strong leader, as someone who was well liked and respected by my teachers and peers. That mattered a great deal to me, and I wanted to keep it that way.

I didn't spend as much time hanging out with the guys from the football team as I did with Hollis, James, Todd, and Drew. But Bullis was a small school, and I still made an effort to be friendly with everyone, to talk to people and get some sense of what mattered to them and why. With my closest friends, I usually talked about politics and literature. But when I was around other groups, whether it was the lacrosse guys or the guys I knew on the football team, I'd try to relate in different ways, by laughing at their jokes and occasionally telling my own.

This sort of balancing act wasn't easy, and despite my efforts, I wasn't able to relate to everyone as much as I would have liked to. At Bullis, I recognized how easily black identity could be distorted. If a black student was in honors or AP classes, he or she was thought of as either exceptional or unqualified. If a black student played lacrosse or hung out with lacrosse players, his or her blackness was questioned. I valued my standing at Bullis, so I felt a certain pressure to act prudently, to avoid being typecast. As a result, I overanalyzed things, such as whom I sat with at lunch and how much time I spent talking with various groups.

I was cool with everyone, but I wasn't happy. I didn't feel that I was enjoying high school or gaining nearly as much as I was putting in. A part of me always wanted to do more, and I was frustrated by the fact that I couldn't. Yet another part of me wanted to relax, to decompress, to fall down and pause and reflect for a while before hustling to get back on my feet again. I felt I was searching for a deeper meaning, for a greater sense of purpose and value that eluded my grasp at every turn.

There were small things here and there that made me feel good, like when Hollis asked me to read *The Divine Comedy* with him so that we could interpret it together, line by line. Hollis was admired at Bullis, but he didn't socialize much outside of school. So I appreciated the fact that he wanted to spend hours discussing literature with me over the phone. I felt the same way when James and his family invited me to go with them to the Anti-Defamation League's annual Concert Against Hate. What mattered to me wasn't so much the invite or the event itself but the fact that James's dad invited me because he recognized my "budding passion for social justice and civil rights."

But these few uplifting gestures were overshadowed by the stress and pressure I felt on a day-to-day basis. It was as if my head space required a certain level of mental gymnastics for me to stay above water, let alone perform well. Being dependable, likable, and high achieving at Bullis meant that whatever might have been bothering me outside of school had to cease to exist in my own mind the moment I walked into my first class. It could be my mom's last voice mail or a physical altercation or threat made by someone I knew I'd see again on the bus. It could be my financial circumstances or water leaking over my bed. Or it could be a combination of all those things and more.

No matter the case, in class and in the hallways, I had to appear happy, composed, and fully present. I had to be on my A game. I had to feel useful, resourceful, and quick on my feet. Because whenever I faltered or didn't meet "my usual standards," it felt to me as if I had nothing to feel good about. Sometimes I couldn't help but wonder how much better I would have been had my life been different, had my desire to overcome my past not driven me to act on so many layers of data and circumspection.

Shortly after starting junior year, I noticed that I hadn't seen Devon hanging out in the hallways or driving around with Kelly in her Range Rover. The next time I saw Anton, Devon's friend from the football team, I approached him. "What's up, man, where's Devon?" I asked. "I haven't seen him in a while."

Class had just let out, and Anton was sitting on the ground with his back against the wall of windows at the far end of the hallway in Bullis's North Hall, home to most of the Upper School's classrooms. He shook his head and looked up at me, disappointed. "He got caught on some shit and had to leave," he said.

"What happened?" This wasn't the first

time I'd heard of an athlete being suspended or even expelled. Bullis was pretty strict about academic and ethical standards. "Was it his grades?"

"Nah," he said, "he got caught fucking Kelly in the wrestling room."

I asked a few other people over the next week or so. They all said it was probably because Devon was failing or had been caught stealing calculators from empty classrooms and the school store to sell at a pawnshop in Rockville. But I wondered if Anton was right. I knew one thing for sure — if Devon had gotten expelled for being caught with Kelly, she hadn't suffered the same fate. I still saw her around all the time, sometimes hanging out with other guys on the football team.

This made me even more cautious about how I talked to girls at Bullis. I was friends with some white girls. I was friendly with everyone. But I made sure to spend time with them only in public or in a group. I considered what people might have thought if I'd dated a white girl I was interested in or asked her to homecoming. I'm sure many students would hardly think twice about it, but I wasn't so sure about certain parents and teachers. Despite my interest in girls of different races at Bullis, I never pursued a relationship with any of them. On a few occasions, I'd even been asked to come over to a girl's house after school to study together or to go to a party she was throwing on the weekend. Though I often wanted to, I always came up with an excuse to say no.

My mom had first taught me about respectability politics — the pressure on blacks to alter their behavior to earn the respect of whites — back when I was at GPA. Years later, her advice on how to carry myself had led me to a book called *Righteous Discontent* by Evelyn Brooks Higginbotham. By the time I was a junior at Bullis, I'd read a good bit about respectability politics and what it meant for black people to seek the acceptance and approval of their white counterparts.

I knew that respectability politics was just another way of surviving and resisting the effects of racism. I knew that in the American imagination, fantasy and fascination could envelope the foreign and forbidden. As much as I may have resented it at times, the reality of racism meant that, if I cared about my own success, I had no choice but to seek the approval of whites and care what they thought of me. My mother had drilled into me that, in order to be accepted, I had to neutralize certain fears and anxieties. That meant constantly monitoring how I sounded, how I looked, and especially how I presented myself.

Yet I was also aware of the fact that in the black community, respectability politics was often seen as being at odds with what it meant to be "authentically black." To me, there was no such thing as being authentically black. Of course, being seen as "authentically white" wasn't something my white peers had to concern themselves with. By then, I'd been around black people of all types — black athletes, black poets, black academics, and black criminals. Yet I had cousins who'd told me I sounded white when we were little. I'd seen my friends' parents look surprised when I said that I enjoyed listening to classical music.

No white person at Bullis had to tell me that his or her perceptions of race were shrouded by unacknowledged fear and curiosity. But everything my mom told me and all the things I'd read about race had made me painfully aware of the myths and stereotypes that reduced black people to objects of fear, hatred, curiosity, and desire. My mother's influence had amplified these things in my mind. So I did my best to steer clear of anything that might confirm someone's tacit suspicions.

But I was a normal teenage boy who was interested in girls. I had no intention of becoming a monk. One day about halfway through the year, I was at Chipotle on the weekend with a friend when we saw a cute girl of mixed race eating with some friends. My friend dared me to ask for her number, so I approached her, introduced myself, and talked to her for a little while. Her name was Noel. She gave me her number, and I made a point of staying in touch.

Noel was great — beautiful, smart, classy, and sweet. She went to a local high school in Maryland, and I felt I could just be myself when I was with her. We dated off and on for a couple of months. It was never anything serious, but there was always the potential for things to blossom. At least, that's how I saw it. I liked the idea of talking about deep subjects on the phone and over text, but she was more interested in having fun.

One Friday night, we went to dinner and then went to the library on a whim to see if they had a book I needed for a school project. We ended up hanging out there for a bit, playing around and sneaking up on each other as we picked up different books and then returned them to the shelves. We were on the bottom floor, and the library was about to close, so it was quiet down there. It felt as if we were alone. With the sun going down outside, the stacks were dim.

I glanced at Noel and flashed my eyebrows. She winked back, nibbling on her lip, as her chin rested in her hands, her lower eyelids resembling crescent-shaped curves. Then I turned my back to her as I perused one of the bookshelves. Noel snuck up behind me and started kissing the side of my neck. I turned to face her, and we kissed more deeply. The moment felt right, and, alone in between those stacks on an almost empty floor, I thought it would be my first time. She leaned back against the bookshelf, and I could hear the lilt in her voice as my hand moved up her inner thigh. Her legs pressed against mine as we kissed.

And then I froze, all hope of what was to come now lost in the dark, trying to find its way out into the light. I sighed, feeling I'd lost my window, as if I'd hit a wall or gotten stuck and lost my clarity. Noel hadn't noticed. Her hands were unbuckling my belt as I began to perspire, wishing the thought of my mother would fade away like some distant apparition that could be ignored or forgotten. I kissed Noel again and told her that I wasn't sure I was ready. She was cool with it, but things fizzled out between us soon after.

Even then, my mother was like gravity for me, an invisible, heavy weight that pulled me down, no matter how hard I tried to resist it. In my report cards, my teachers referred to me as "the perfect young man" and "a rarity — an intellectual who possesses a poet's heart and an activist's passion." I'd won the Citizenship Award and the Outstanding Service Award at the end of my sophomore year at Bullis for being such a strong and ethical student leader. None of my friends or teachers, and certainly not Noel, had any clue what was going through my mind most of the time. But the truth is that my mom's impact on me was an obstacle that I worried about more than I ever let on. I resented my mom for this. But I never told anyone how it made me feel.

Soon after, James's parents invited me to spend the weekend at their bay house in Roanoke, Virginia. It was one of three homes that James's family had on the East Coast. This one had six bedrooms in the main house, a guesthouse, a pool house, and a six-car garage with basketball and tennis courts on opposite ends of the six-acre property. I was used to visiting the homes of wealthy friends, but this mansion was one of the most luxurious I'd ever seen.

Over dinner outside on their bluestone patio, James's parents bragged about me to some of their friends. "He's just the nicest young man; he's like our adopted son," James's mom said. "He's going to be president one day, I'm telling you. He reads all these books and remembers them all. I don't know how he reads so many."

I smiled warmly, as everyone around the glass-top aluminum outdoor table looked at me with piqued curiosity. "We should get him to help Anna with her student government speech. He's a terrific writer."

"Happy to help whenever I can. You guys are like family," I said.

"I told him to call me Mom," James's mother said affectionately. She paused and smiled at her friends. "Zach is going to go to Harvard, and he's going to win the Potomac Youth of the Year Award."

I'd put unreasonably high expectations on myself, and now I struggled under the weight of those intentions. All the while, my ability to cope with everything outside of school felt diminished and near exhausted. I'd pushed through everything for so long without complaint, but a part of me still felt like I'd underachieved, like I hadn't done enough, like I was living just to prove that I could be of greater value to those around me. That, in some sense, was the only thing that got me up every morning at 4:45 to catch the bus.

One person I felt I could talk to a little bit during this difficult time was my English teacher, Mr. Kinder. He was young — in his late twenties — and felt sort of like an older brother. He gave me his best advice about whatever I asked him. One day I was in Mr. Kinder's class when Dr. Boarman, the Bullis headmaster, stuck his head into the classroom and gestured for me to come over to him. I got up and walked out into the hallway. Dr. Boarman was standing there with an older, handsome couple.

"Zach, I would like you to meet Mr. and Mrs. Johnson," he said, and I shook their hands. "I want you to tell them what you think of Bullis," he told me. "Tell them about the diversity here and how you feel different groups interact with each other. You can be honest," he said, giving me a friendly pat on the shoulder.

I knew what Dr. Boarman expected me to say, and I didn't hesitate. He'd pulled me out of class for similar reasons once or twice before, and he did so again later that year.

"Bullis is a place where you'll meet people from a variety of backgrounds," I said smoothly. "Even more so, it's not just that diversity exists. I've built relationships with peers who do a variety of things, from theater to academic decathlon to football. We have a community where the diversity we have does not create tensions. It creates bonds that are of value to the students."

Dr. Boarman looked on with a proud smile. "I've got to tell you," he said to the Johnsons, "Zach here memorizes long passages and can quote them at the drop of a hat. I've never seen anything like it. He's one of our best and brightest." The well-groomed couple shook my hand again and told me what a pleasure it had been to meet me, and I went back to class.

Soon after, the administration chose me as one of the students to be profiled and highlighted on the Bullis website. Some of the most prominent students from each grade were featured, and Todd, Hollis, and I were selected to represent our year. For the photo shoot to go along with my profile, I walked down to the Blair Family Center for the Arts. I had my pictures taken and was interviewed about the clubs I was involved in and what I appreciated about Bullis. I was asked again to comment on

226

the school's diversity.

When the profile went up soon after on the Bullis website, I brought my laptop downstairs so that my grandma could see it on my computer. She had finally retired from her job as a janitor, and her mobility was getting worse. She had to pause on each step whenever she walked upstairs. So whenever possible, we tried to make sure she didn't have to get up and walk around. In our small, cluttered living room, she leaned against the table for balance as I pulled the profile up on the screen. "Oh, look at you!" she said with a joyful laugh that made me smile.

But even then, I felt I wasn't living up to my own expectations. Mr. Eist, the learning specialist who ran the student tutoring program, was a visionary who cared deeply about his work, and he wanted to create hundreds of short videos and podcasts for the Bullis website, teaching various topics, from historical concepts to grammatical rules and how to solve quadratic equations. Mr. Eist had seen how good I was at explaining these concepts to the students I tutored, and he asked me to create as many podcasts as I could.

I was drained. I had no more to give. Yet I wanted to be admired, and that meant saying yes even when I wanted to say no. I agreed enthusiastically, despite the fact that I was already spread so thin, and knew that this would be a heavy undertaking.

I was already tutoring up to ten students a week, holding several leadership positions in the school, and maintaining an A average in all AP and honors courses. I'd even given up my study hall that year to take another AP course. I gave up that study hall because I wanted to prove that I could excel with an unusually rigorous course load. But with my commute and personal circumstances, it was a lot to manage, especially given that I always wanted to read more than I had to for most of my classes. I wanted to be prepared for the times in my history and English classes when my teachers would look to me when a student stumped them with a difficult question. "Keep me honest, Zach," Mr. Kinder once told me before a class discussion about Ralph Waldo Emerson. This kind of recognition meant a lot to me, and I'd be damned if I wasn't going to do all that I could to stand and deliver when called upon to do so.

After only a couple of weeks, Mr. Eist stopped me in the hallway. "Dr. Wood" — as he often called me — "how are we doing with the podcasts?" I told him that I'd only been able to make two so far and I didn't have access to the software at home, so I had to stay at Bullis even later than usual to get them done. "Oh, all right, man," he said, but I could see the hint of disappointment in his eyes. "When do you think you'll have time to do more?"

I wanted to help as many people as I could, but I also wanted to help Mr. Eist in particular because his goal wasn't to sweet-talk wealthy parents into donating money for the school or to priggishly monitor the halls in between classes to reprimand students who were slightly out of uniform. Mr. Eist didn't pretend to be anything other than what he was: a creative learning specialist who was dedicated to improving the academic achievement of his students. To be the student and leader that I wanted to be, I felt that I had to follow through.

At the same time, I wondered what people would think if I stopped making all the extra effort, dropped the facade, and showed everyone how I really felt. Everyone at Bullis knew only the things about me that I wanted them to know, which represented a small sliver of my actual experience. What would happen if that ratio were reversed — if instead of the guy who quoted Plato, held leadership positions, and helped students with their papers, I was nothing more than an average kid from Bellevue?

Ultimately, I had so little in my life to feel good about or look forward to. I didn't have a big house or even a comfortable house, a family name that meant something, or a guaranteed future by virtue of who my folks were. My mom was a source of pain and conflict. My dad worked hard and loved me, but I couldn't get ten words out of him when I asked any question with a level of depth. We could talk about sports and sometimes what was on the news, but nothing thoughtful or reflective. No emotion, no weakness, no vulnerability, ever. I knew that was how he dealt with challenges. But what did I have to feel good about? It all stemmed from being hardworking, productive, helpful, and high achieving. That was it.

By the time junior year ended, college visits and applications had become priority number one. Where did we want to go, and what could we do to give ourselves the best chance of getting in? My friends all had family contacts, legacies, and parents who would help them navigate the admissions process. I was on my own, but I was used to that.

I was at James's house one night over the summer, talking about college. I knew that

James wanted to go to Brown. "I know some folks there," I told James. "I'll talk to them and see if they have any advice for you about the process." I had some contacts from various conferences I'd gone to, and this was one way I could help James, a student who already did very well academically on his own.

Earlier in the summer, I'd sent one of Hollis's poems to Reginald Dwayne Betts, who had stayed in touch with me. Dwayne had become a close mentor. He was someone I could be real with, the only person who knew that there were days when I came home from school and wanted to punch a hole in the wall. Dwayne understood why I felt that way, often without my even having to explain why. But my connection at Brown wasn't like my connection to Dwayne; it was to a former professor whom I'd met once and didn't know well enough to ask that kind of favor of.

That night, I was on my way home from James's house waiting for the bus at Anacostia. It was dark and humid outside. I was leaning against the advertisement on the bus bay, reading an article on my phone. There were people around, waiting at various spots along the bus terminal, but not too many. Though I was looking at my phone, I was vigilant. Always listening, glancing up often to survey my surroundings.

Behind me was a group of guys I'd seen before but never interacted with. The four of them were always together, usually chilling in the lot behind the newspaper stands. But that day they were wildin' out. They looked a few years older than me. All with tattoos, chains, and one with dreads. I'd overheard enough of their conversation to glean that he was the kingpin.

"Aye, look at that nigga with the backpack young, ha-ha, he look like what's his name, uh," I heard one of them say behind me, to the right.

"Ha-ha-ha! Nah, Bob, hold up. I seen this li'l nigga before. This the nigga who told twelve I was moving bricks. Had them patting me down and shit. Li'l bitch-ass nigga about to get clapped quick."

This was the kind of situation I'd narrowly escaped a few times before. But in those cases, the affront was more of a test to see how I'd respond to being flamed by dudes I didn't know. Would I take it and look weak, or buck up and talk back? Sometimes, I found easy outs in getting off at the next stop and walking, or faking a phone call, or moving to an area packed with more people.

232

Other times, I was able to defuse the situation. But these dudes were different. I sensed that they were the kind of guys who'd roll up on somebody and pull out a gun in broad daylight. Had I seen them do it? No. But I'd been around enough people in this area to separate the trash talkers quick to throw hands from the niggas who had tattoos on their necks and gun grips sticking out of their waistbands. I knew I'd see these guys again, too. So I had to judge carefully whether to run, fight, cooperate, or try to talk my way out of it.

"Look at this nigga's teeth son, his shit got wrecked," one of them said to another as they flanked me.

"You ain't from round here, nigga, not with that backpack on like that. What, you get your tooth knocked out, nigga, you got beat, huh?" They all laughed.

I was scared, but I knew better than to panic or show fear. So I replied, "I don't want any problems, man, just trying to stay in my lane."

"Ha-ha-ha, bop!" he said, as he faked like he was going to punch me. I flinched instinctively, throwing my left arm up to cover my face as I clinched my right fist. Then he shoved me hard. I stumbled back and hit the hard plastic enclosing the bus bay, recovering quickly to regain my balance. I didn't know what was coming next, so I put both hands up and said, "Listen, I'm not trying to fight y'all, man, just going about my business."

Seconds later, he teed off at my jaw. From there, everything devolved quickly.

I had managed to weave his first punch enough so that it grazed the top of my head. And I covered up as best I could, but after his third or fourth punch, I fell to the ground. None of his punches landed directly on my face, but I had braces and a wire sticking out in two places that needed to be cut, so it didn't take much for my mouth to start bleeding. Once I fell to the ground, I got kicked twice before the bus squeaked to the curb and came to a halt. Luckily, they scattered. Once I saw them hop the fence and run toward Barry Farm, I hopped up and grabbed my backpack.

I boarded the bus, feeling the cut inside my lip and across my gums with my tongue, thinking about how badly that could have turned out had the bus come just a few minutes later.

When I got home, I tried to cut the wire with scissors, but that didn't work because the scissors were too large and awkwardly shaped to fit in my mouth. So I found a fingernail clipper, scrubbed it with soap, and used that to fix the wire as best I could. I'd missed my last few appointments with the orthodontist because we didn't have the money to pay for previous visits. But I knew that I would have to go back soon. By this time, my dad knew that I'd been in scuffles at Anacostia, but I didn't bother telling him the details. He never complained, no matter what he faced, and I wanted my dad to think that I was man enough to get around by myself without his having to worry about me.

Over the next few weeks, college was the hot topic, and I knew James was waiting for the information I'd promised him. I told him I'd reach out to my contact and ask him to send James some information. But once I said that, I felt trapped. James would expect me to deliver. And I was glad he trusted my ability to help him with a process so important to us both. More than anything, I knew how much it would mean to James to hear from someone at Brown, and I genuinely wanted to help.

That night, I sat at the desk in my room and tried to figure out what to do. While I can try to explain my reasoning, the truth is that the decision I made was not rational and thus cannot be rationalized. It represents a singular moment in which, under stress and pressure, my thinking was psychologically amiss. At the time, however, my reasoning was that I had three options: I could e-mail the professor and ask him to help James. I could tell James that I'd misled him and couldn't really help. Or I could fudge it. None of these options felt right. And none of them would be easy. But only one of them, I believed, would allow me to maintain the relationships and the respect I'd worked so hard to build.

I went into Gmail and created a new account. Then I wrote an e-mail to James with some advice on how to apply to Brown and signed it from the professor. I also included a line about how lucky James was to have me as a friend. I didn't feel good about it. It wasn't honest, and it wasn't that smart, but I figured I'd send the one e-mail and be done with it. What harm would that do?

A few days later, James invited me over. When I got to his house, his mother welcomed me with a warm hug. "Zach, thank you so, so much for putting James in contact with the professor," she told me. James and his family thought the advice the professor had given him was brilliant, and he replied, asking more questions. I should have stopped then and admitted to what I'd done. But I didn't. I didn't see an easy way out of it, so instead I replied and sent more e-mails.

When Hollis and Drew heard about what I'd done for James, I sensed that they would have appreciated it if I did the same type of thing for them, if not expected me to. To this day, if there was one thing in my life that I could do over, it would be sending those e-mails. Yet I did it again. I created fake e-mail addresses from people from different institutions, and I sent advice to Hollis and to Drew.

Over the next couple of weeks there was a deep rift between my discomfort about what I was doing and the way my friends' and their parents' reactions made me feel. I'd earned their respect a while before, and I knew they liked me a lot — or the version of me they knew — but now they fully embraced me, as if I were family. It was a subtle difference that penetrated my every interaction with them and made it hard for me to put a stop to what I'd started. Simply put, they loved me for what I'd done, and I'll admit it — it felt good to be loved.

CHAPTER 8
CIRCLING

It didn't take long for my sense of what was right to cut through the cloud of respect, admiration, and appreciation that sending those e-mails had created. I let them peter out as quickly as I could, within a few weeks of sending the first one. No one had gotten hurt, and I believed this temporary though terrible error in judgment was behind me.

I spent the rest of the summer at the five-week classics program at St. John's College in New Mexico. I wanted to master the Western canon and was intrigued by the program's small seminars with students of various ages. My mentor, Reginald Dwayne Betts, helped me fund-raise the tuition money and even said he'd put down a thousand dollars if we couldn't raise the full amount. He advised me to create a Go-FundMe account, and once I did, he shared the page with his contacts, helping me raise more than $1,500. There was no way I would have been able to attend the program if it weren't for Dwayne, and I was extremely grateful.

I loved it at St. John's. It was intellectual heaven, and when the administration offered me the option of skipping my senior year of high school to enroll there immediately, I seriously considered it. For a while, I'd felt as if I were putting more into my experience at Bullis than I was getting out of it. This would give me a chance to dive right into something more rigorous and, hopefully, rewarding.

Coincidentally, my English teacher, Mr. Kinder, was attending a graduate program at St. John's at the same time I was there, and I talked the decision over with him. While we were in New Mexico, I spent a lot of time with Mr. Kinder, and I ended up confiding in him about some things no one else at Bullis knew about, including some of the challenges I faced at home and my recent altercation at the bus stop. I told him about the financial strain that paying our portion of my tuition placed on my dad. The tuition at Bullis went up each year, but my scholarship didn't increase by the same percentage. I told Mr. Kinder that I might have to get a job in the fall to help bridge that gap.

When I told Mr. Kinder that I was considering staying at St. John's, he reminded me that if I stayed on and graduated from Bullis, I'd have a good chance of going to a top college, where I'd find even greater opportunities and rewards than at St. John's. He also told me how much I mattered at Bullis; how respected, valued, and admired I was; and how much I'd be missed if I left. This was ultimately what convinced me. I decided to take his advice and started my senior year intending to make the most of it before moving on to college.

Early in the year, I was walking down the hall when I passed the principal, Mr. Delinsky. He was a very present principal — always responsive to students and engaged in what was going on at Bullis. On campus, Mr. Delinsky had a disarmingly delightful demeanor. He was gentle, warm, soft-spoken, and very approachable. He'd even seen me sitting at the bus stop once and offered to give me a ride to the nearest Metro station. To that point, I'd believed Mr. Delinsky to be the most virtuous person I would ever meet. So when he saw me that day and asked me to come see him in his office whenever I had a chance, I wasn't worried, though I had no clue what he might have wanted.

I walked to his office in North Hall after class. Mr. Delinsky welcomed me with a smile and asked me to sit in one of the plush chairs across from his desk. "Zach," he began, looking concerned, "Mr. Kinder told me that some people on the bus were threatening you, that you'd been injured in a fight and might be in danger." He went on to describe the incident and how I had told Mr. Kinder that my grandmother had been robbed and that I had tried to save her.

That wasn't exactly right — obviously, some information had been mangled in translation — but I didn't want to contradict or interrupt him, so I sat tight and waited to hear what he was going to say next. "The thing is" — he paused and steepled his fingers together — "I talked to your father, and he didn't seem to know about any of this." He frowned, looking sorry for me. "I told Mr. Kinder that you must have exaggerated some things."

I was ticked. I didn't know where to begin. If he were not my principal, I would have kept it simple: "Listen, I don't entertain assumptions when the respectful thing to do is ask questions. What goes on in my personal life is my business and whom I choose to share things with is my prerogative. I'll show myself out. Be well." But Mr. Delinsky was my principal, and I understood the implications of institutions having power over you. So I didn't bother clarifying what had actually happened or explaining my dad's response. I stayed quiet and let him continue.

"Let me give you my pop-psychology analysis of what's happening here, Zach," he said. He lowered his eyes with practiced sympathy. "I know your mom has a mental illness," he told me. "I know the experiences you had with her may have been tragic, and I've done a lot of reading about what dealing with a lack of empathy during childhood can do to someone's life. I'd love to help you find a therapist to deal with your stress and talk about whatever may be going on in your life."

I felt my jaw tighten. Since I'd arrived, I had largely avoided talking about my mother with anyone at Bullis. Her name didn't appear on my application, and she had nothing to do with my experience there. I hadn't even told Mr. Kinder much about her. Despite whatever Mr. Delinsky thought he knew, he understood very little about my life. He may have read some studies about empathy, but this was a man who acted so pure and innocent that I doubted he'd survive for five minutes in Anacostia. He knew nothing about what I faced when I exited the Bullis gates every evening, and he knew nothing about my past. So, no, I wasn't interested in his pop psychoanalysis or in receiving his "help."

Yet I was keenly aware of my position. There was no question of who in that room held all the power. I knew that power was something that showed itself in a number of different ways. On the bus, it was the guy who could get me to give him my seat. At school, it was the principal, who could summon me to his office and make me agree to see a therapist. It didn't matter what the power looked like. I knew how to recognize it, and when I did, I knew when to resist and when to submit.

I thought briefly about explaining to him that my dad and I had a clear understanding that people at Bullis weren't supposed to know about certain realities and challenges we faced, partly because I didn't want them to. I thought about explaining to him why telling my father about how guys had run up on me because I didn't look hard felt worse than walking up to my football coach and saying, "I got a cut on my elbow from that last hit. Can you help me find a Band-Aid?" But I didn't owe him an explanation, and as I saw it, unless something in my private life was affecting my ability to show up and do my best at school, it was none of Mr. Delinsky's concern.

"Thanks for your concern. It seems like there's been some miscommunication, and I'm sorry for that," I said, maintaining my resolve. I agreed to go to therapy, to check in frequently with Mr. Delinsky, and to keep him abreast of how my sessions were going. But shortly after I left his office, I e-mailed my contact at St. John's to see if their offer still stood. There was no way I was going to allow the principal to be involved in my life this way or to put my father in a position where he had to listen to this man tell him what to do.

Over the next week, Mr. Delinsky kept close tabs on me — how I was doing in every class, which friends I was spending time with, and so on. Just a little more than a week after our meeting, I was talking with a teacher in North Hall when Mr. Delinsky came up. "Zach, come to my office right away," he interrupted. This was not the amiable way he'd asked me to stop by last time. *What now?* I wondered as I walked down the hall to his office.

I paused as I entered Mr. Delinsky's office. He was sitting behind his desk with his back toward the door. Beside him was Ms. Chehak, looking concerned. On the other side of the room was the school psychologist, whom I'd never spoken to, aside from saying hello in the hallway. And, seated in one of the beige chairs across from Mr. Delinsky's desk, looking ill at ease, was my dad. I tried to catch his eye as I lowered myself into the other chair, but he was staring off into the distance.

Before anyone said a word, Mr. Delinsky spun around to face us with a stack of papers in his hand. He put the papers down on the desk in front of me. With a quick glance, I could see what they were. Mr. Delinsky placed both of his hands flat on the desk. "Zach, did you write these e-mails?" he asked.

It was still early in the year — technically summer — and despite the air-conditioning in the office, it was hot. I was sweating. "No, can you give me a moment to speak to my father?" I knew that if I could have just a minute with him, we could figure this out. He could speak up and say that it had just been a prank or explain all the pressure I was under. No one had been hurt, and the e-mails had all been sent from my home computer two months before, over the summer, entirely outside the school's jurisdiction. I was sure that if we acted strategically they would let it slide or give me a small slap on the wrist. I'd never done anything even close to requiring disciplinary action before.

"No, Zach, that's not going to happen," Mr. Delinsky said. I looked at my dad with my eyes wide and my eyebrows raised, hoping he'd get the message and insist on having a chance to speak to me alone. But he just stared ahead, looking defeated, as if any sense of power or agency had been completely drained from him. Then Mr. Delinsky spoke again. "Zach," he said, "it'll be a lot easier if you just tell the truth."

"Yes," I said finally. "I apologize. I'm very sorry." Ms. Chehak looked worried, as if she knew that there was no choice but for me to get skinned alive. I didn't have time to wonder why she was even there in the first place.

"You're going to go on an immediate medical leave," Mr. Delinsky said. Ms. Chehak looked deeply saddened. My dad looked like he was in a pressure cooker. The school psychologist stared ahead impassively. But now that he'd said it, Mr. Delinsky visibly relaxed. He sat back in his chair. "You've probably dealt with a lot of things in your life that made you feel insecure, Zach," he told me. "And sending those e-mails made you feel like you had some power."

What I wanted to say to Mr. Delinsky in that moment was this: "No, sir, make no mistake. I was never under the illusion that I had any power." Instead, I capitulated completely, apologizing profusely and taking full responsibility for what I'd done.

With that, my dad and I got in his car and drove home. I felt disgraced. For three years, I had done everything I could to be of value to the Bullis community, to be a model student and a strong leader, and to never give anyone any possible reason to be upset with me. I skipped meals, gave up sleep, and even put myself in the hospital trying to fill this void. And on my insatiable quest to earn everyone's admiration, with a handful of fake e-mails, I'd managed to erase the respect and goodwill I'd fought so hard to earn.

My dad was silent. He didn't admonish me at all. Between us lay the unspoken understanding that this mistake was mine to own and mine to regret. It was for me to be disappointed in myself. And I was.

After an hour of driving, we pulled up in front of our small house. It was quiet outside, and I could hear the pound of a basketball hitting the pavement on a nearby court. For the first time since I'd entered Mr. Delinsky's office, my dad looked at me. "Everyone makes mistakes, and you've dealt with worse than this," he told me. "You'll figure it out."

As always, my dad had managed to say so little and yet so much. He meant to be supportive, and I appreciated that, but his words of encouragement did little more than remind me of how alone I really was.

Mr. Delinsky had instructed me to apologize to James, Hollis, and Drew the next day, after he'd had a chance to tell them what happened. Drew responded emotionally at first, but once he had a chance to absorb everything, he calmed down and seemed to forgive me. James was gracious and told me how much he appreciated my apology. But Hollis never responded.

I was slated to speak at an upcoming Bullis event about what it meant to be a scholar. The day after I went on medical leave, I spoke to Mr. Delinsky on the phone. "Out of respect, I wouldn't mind if you chose to use a different speaker," I told him.

"Let's wait and see what happens," he responded. I wasn't sure what that meant. What exactly were the factors that would determine my fate?

I heard back from Mr. Delinsky two days later. "You have a choice to make," he told me over the phone. "This can go before the conduct review board. Then one of three things will happen. You could get a short suspension, you could get a long suspension, or you risk expulsion." He paused. "I have to be honest with you," he said. "I don't know which one of these is the most likely, but the chances are small that you'll get expelled."

"But there's a chance?" I asked. I couldn't believe that sending some e-mails would result in expulsion, but if there was any possibility of it, I knew right away that this was not a risk I wanted to take.

"Yes," Mr. Delinsky responded.

"And if I'm suspended, I'll have to explain that to colleges?"

"Yes," he said again. It was starting to look like any of these three possible outcomes could ruin my chance of getting into a top school. "The other option," he continued, "is that you withdraw."

I sat back in the wobbly plastic chair at the desk in my bedroom. "And I can do that on my own terms?" Mr. Delinsky had presented two options, but it was clear that it wasn't really a choice at all.

"Yes."

"Will I still have access to my records and college counselors?" The ax had fallen, and now I was trying to salvage what I could from the remains. When Mr. Delinsky agreed to these requests, I told him, "I'll withdraw within the hour."

There was a pause. In the silence I could almost hear Mr. Delinsky nodding. "Zach," he said, "would you mind telling me why you sent those e-mails?"

He sounded sincere, and I answered honestly. "I wanted my friends to value me and see that I could help them. I didn't think it would damage them or hurt their chances in any way, but I understand that it corroded their trust in me. I had no intention of hurting anyone," I told him. "I just wanted to help."

Mr. Delinsky seemed satisfied. "I think this will be for the best," he told me. "I'm just glad we didn't have to get the police involved."

Once I told my dad what was happening, he said nothing about how to transfer or find a way to graduate. It was on me to figure out how to move on from this. It was too late to register at a different high school, so I started looking at online high schools and ended up transferring to Excel High School online.

My focus, though, was on learning from this, on figuring out how to earn back what I'd lost and to bounce back better and stronger and more admirable than ever. I'd been caught, punished, and exposed, and that fueled a burning frustration and desire to prove once and for all that I didn't need my mom, the people at Bullis, or anyone else. I could make it on my own; I *would* make it on my own.

I thought about all the things teenagers normally get in trouble for and how I'd never done any of them. I'd never tried alcohol. I'd never done drugs. I'd never done anything sexually reckless or ill advised; I didn't even date a single girl at Bullis. I'd never skipped a single class or gone home and said, "Screw my homework." I'd never cheated on a test or plagiarized a paper.

I thought about all the effort I'd put in over the last three years, all the sacrifices I'd made. The late hours up working. The sleepless nights. The four-hour, two-way commute. The time I spent preparing for Model UN conferences and tutoring people in the library after school. I thought about how I'd poured everything I had into putting my best foot forward every day, despite the obstacles I'd faced.

Sending those e-mails wasn't just wrong; it was immoral and willfully dishonest. And I'd never felt worse about anything I'd done in my entire life. Yet there was a part of me that could not help but think that if I had been white and wealthy, I would have graduated from Bullis. Instead, I missed out on senior projects, on senior homecoming, and on senior prom; and on graduation day, I didn't walk across the stage with all the peers whose respect I'd worked so hard to earn. I had made a terrible mistake. And there were tough consequences. So I resolved to deal with them just as I had every other obstacle.

Alone in my bedroom, I reread biographies and memoirs of some of the men I most admired — Martin Luther King, Frederick Douglass, Bill Clinton, Reginald Dwayne Betts, Ulysses S. Grant, Franklin Delano Roosevelt, Barack Obama, Cornel West, Henry Louis Gates, and Kobe Bryant. I was searching these texts for clues about how the men I aspired to be like had confronted their own failures. Each of these people had overcome something unique. The common link between all their stories was that their strength ultimately came down to resilience. I knew that to be strong and resilient like them, I had to refuse to let my worst moments have the last word.

Reading about Kobe Bryant in particular inspired me to commit to everything I put my mind to the way he committed to basketball. I grew determined to be more efficient, precise, and aggressive, to concentrate on what I wanted and, most important, to go about it according to my principles. Kobe had always been my favorite basketball player, and I had a deep respect for the way he approached the game. For him, it was all or nothing. His coach, Phil Jackson, said that if he set the bar at a seven, Kobe would raise it to a nine. No matter what he was facing off the court, he showed up and refused to give anything less than his absolute best.

This was the mind-set I wanted to bring to everything I took on. At the end of the day, if all I had was the fact that I'd worked as hard as possible at something I cared about, that was something to be proud of. From that point on, I wanted to do everything I could to help as many people as I could, but I would do only what I was capable of doing. I recognized that I had hurt my friends in part because of who I was to them. They had trust in our relationships, and my actions had broken that trust. I had to sit with that.

Over the next few months, I spent some part of every day thinking about what I'd done and why I'd done it. I saw that I'd been searching for something to feel good about, and that it would have been better for me to deal with those feelings honestly instead of making them disappear by doing more and more and committing to doing more than I actually could. Through my reading and introspection, I learned what qualities I most admired: understanding and caring about how what you do, what you say, and even how you think affect people.

I had always been trying to grow intellectually, but now I realized that if I truly wanted to help people, I had to resist the impulse to see things abstractly and focus on the humans behind the data. My thoughts had also impacted my friends as a result of all the judgments and assumptions I'd made about them. They never told me that I had to do all those things to earn their respect. I had taken them all on willingly and then resented them for it. All this forced me to reconcile who I was with who I wanted to be, and face the fact that I wasn't there yet.

Going forward, I would act on my principles and my instincts and push myself to do what Kobe Bryant always did, which was use the pressures and challenges and obstacles in life not as something to run from but as something to overcome; to see every instance of self-doubt and self-contempt as an opportunity to rise above it and be better than I was before.

Academically, online high school was easy, so I spent most of my time doing my own reading — delving into subjects such as physics and the history of science, which I knew the least about, so that I could learn more — and escaping from the house whenever I could. Since I'd moved to DC, putting all my energy into my life at Bullis was the only thing that had kept me going. Now I didn't have that or any of the typical senior-year events or activities to look forward to. I'd lost my closest friends and the teachers I'd considered mentors. But I'd be damned if I was going to sit around feeling sorry for myself.

My cousin DA, who went to high school in Virginia, was a phenomenal baseball player who was having a hard time in school. He had an amazing opportunity to go to an all-star tournament, but he didn't have the money, and there was some question of whether he was going to graduate from high school. I went down to Virginia and stayed with him for two weeks. During that time, I spoke at his high school, helped him with his schoolwork, and started a Go-FundMe account to raise money for the tournament. When he still came up short, I gave him three hundred dollars from my own pocket that I'd earned doing odd jobs for Mrs. Brown and some other neighbors. I did not want to see him miss that opportunity.

When I had done all I could for DA, I went back on the road, visiting another cousin, named RC, in New York and a friend from Bullis who had graduated the year before and was at the University of Pennsylvania, and doing fly-in programs to visit a number of colleges — Williams, Swarthmore, Brandeis, Amherst, and some other schools that I wasn't even interested in attending. I just didn't want to be at home. On these campuses, I had access to extensive libraries and academic journals and could even sit in on classes. This was far more rewarding and enriching than anything I could accomplish at home.

After all these visits, I decided to apply early decision to Williams College. I had good conversations with the admissions people there and valued the individualized attention students received and the sense of community that Williams strived for. It was a small school, and I liked the idea that I could get to know people personally and see those same people around campus daily. If I was accepted, I was determined to be a great friend to the people I met there.

When I was in DC, which was rarely, I spent a lot of time with Nicole. I'd gone to school with kids whose parents were millionaires with degrees from Harvard and Yale. They had lavish lifestyles, ample connections, and auditoriums at Ivy League universities named after their grandparents. My sister, like me, had none of that. She was only in fourth grade at the time, but I wanted more than anything to be there for her in ways that I wished someone had been there for me. I was determined to use my knowledge and experience to help her achieve her dreams and find joy and motivation along the way.

When Nicole was at her mom's house, I hung out with James. He'd forgiven me, but he didn't want to be seen with me in public, so we snuck around. I spent a lot of weekends at his house and was grateful that his parents never once brought up the e-mails. One weekend when I was staying with James we were walking down the street to Chipotle when he yelled, "Duck!" I crouched down behind a bush, knowing that some guys from Bullis were on the other side of the street.

James wasn't the only person I kept in touch with from Bullis. A friend of mine named Ryan had my back and was my eyes and ears after I'd left. When I was at Bullis, Ryan was determined to improve his writing and wasn't afraid to ask for help. I was happy to help him, and that continued after I left. Shortly after, he told me that when the school announced that I'd left for personal reasons, people were shocked. In the room he was in during the announcement, there were gasps. I also kept in touch with Drew and continued helping him with some writing assignments, but our relationship grew increasingly distant.

I was back in New York visiting RC when I got the e-mail that I'd been accepted to Williams. We were planning to see a movie that night, and I was waiting for him in a little pizza place near his job. I'd like to say that I was elated, but more than anything I was heartened and bent on making up for lost time there — developing relationships with professors, making a difference on campus, and finally becoming the leader I wanted to be.

I called my dad to tell him the news. It was mid-December, and I'd been traveling so much that I hadn't seen him since Thanksgiving. But when he picked up the phone and I told him that I'd been accepted to Williams, all he said was, "All right, cool." I hung up the phone and briefly clenched my fist before releasing it onto the table. After all I'd been through and everything I'd accomplished on my own, even the mistakes I'd owned up to, I was under-whelmed by my dad's response. For a moment I wondered if there was anything I could do that would actually make him proud of me.

Later that night, I thought about how my mom might react to this news. Since I'd left her house four years earlier, we'd spoken maybe a dozen times. I hadn't seen her once. Our conversations varied from tense to intense, brief to long and involved. Most of the time, she seemed to want to put everything behind us and act as if we had a normal mother-son relationship. She asked how I was doing in school, if I was dating, and whether or not I was having sex. I vacil-lated between refusing to tell her anything at all and wanting to share every accom-plishment and evidence of normal teenage behavior to prove that she hadn't affected me in all the ways she might have. Now a part of me wanted her to know that I had done it — that, despite the challenges, I'd gotten through high school and would be going to Williams; and, most of all, that I'd done it without her.

I called my mom the next day, and when I told her, she screamed with excitement, "Oh, my God, my son got into Williams! It is the best school. Fuck Harvard!" She told me that she wanted to throw me a party to celebrate. At first, I resisted and said that I'd be willing to see her if she came to DC to visit. But it was clear that she so badly wanted to be a part of my success and show me off to her friends and colleagues back home. Eventually I decided that if she was going to make such a big effort, the least I could do was show up.

I flew to Detroit that February, feeling anxious about seeing her. On the plane, I ran through a million possible scenarios in my mind, all the things that could possibly go wrong and, if they did, how I could avoid being trapped there with her. But as soon as I got to her house, it was obvious that a big effort was being made to make this visit as pleasant as possible. I was happy to play along. We chatted amicably about Williams, and I told her about some summer programs that I was thinking of applying to.

But after a little while, her true nature began to seep through our polite interactions. When I said something positive about DC or my dad, she turned to me with that look in her eyes. I was eighteen then — a man — and in many ways had been living as an adult with grown-up responsibilities since I'd left her home. It wasn't the same as the last time I'd seen her, but I hated the fact that that look still had a small amount of power over me.

The next morning when I came downstairs, she looked up at me from her seat at the kitchen table with a bright smile. It was a crisp winter day, but it was sunny outside. She sat cast in the glow from the window, smoking a cigarette. "Good morning, Zachary," she said, reaching up to pinch my cheek. Without thinking, I flinched, swerving my head to the side to avoid her reach. I was too old for her to pinch my cheeks. But she recoiled, turning away from me with a wounded expression on her face. "I assume you want to feed yourself breakfast," she said bitterly.

I sighed. All in all, the visit had gone better than I'd feared, but there was no escaping the fact that my mom was the same complicated and unpredictable person she had always been. There was potential for our relationship to improve, and I held on to the hope that it would, but it would never be simple.

As the school year drew to a close, I was thinking about the summer. I was used to spending my summers diving into new subjects that I hadn't necessarily studied in detail at school. Now that I was on my way to Williams, I wanted to get a head start on college courses before I got to campus. Knowing that I'd be at a small liberal arts college made me want to experience what it would be like at a big Ivy League university, so I applied to summer programs at Yale, Stanford, Brown, and Georgetown as a visiting student. I was accepted at all of them and faced financial barriers at all of them. Stanford had the best aid policies for visiting students, particularly for their precollege summer session programs, but there still was a big gap between the aid they offered and the amount I could pay.

Determined not to let money get in the way of this opportunity, I set up a Go-FundMe account and reached out to a few contacts to see if they would be willing to help me get the word out. After Bruce Leshan interviewed me for WUSA9, a local news network, about a dozen media outlets followed. Suddenly, my story was everywhere, and viewers responded by making contributions big and small. I was immensely grateful for their support.

An arts patron in DC named Peggy Cooper Cafritz heard about me and ended up footing a huge chunk of the Stanford bill. She made it all possible, in the end. Since then, Peggy has become somewhat like a third grandmother to me — always there for me when I needed her, be it for money or advice, or to bounce off random ideas.

The day I flew to California to attend Stanford, a glowing profile of me appeared in *The Washington Times*. Certain elements of the piece were problematic. It described me as a "neoliberal," sympathetic to conservative ideas, instead of a liberal Democrat, open to engaging the other side. It also took some comments I made about Mitt Romney and Newt Gingrich out of context. That bothered me, the fact that I was misquoted. I also strongly disagreed with an argument the article made against affirmative action and some negative comments it included about leftist professors. But I did appreciate the feature and the reporter's interest in my story. As I boarded the plane, reading the piece, I felt that some of my hard work had paid off.

My summer at Stanford was almost magical. It was the full college experience, living in the dorms and eating in the campus cafeteria. This was a far cry from the four years I'd spent reading in shadowy cramped quarters, and I loved it. Experiencing a totally new learning environment allowed me to grow and enjoy life more than I ever had before. I dated, and I developed some of the most significant, interesting, and meaningful friendships of my life with people I'd give an arm for to this day.

As always, I was ready to learn about some new topics. This time, I focused on subjects such as climate change, alternative energy sources, and ethology. Remembering how Kobe Bryant studied predators to perfect his ability to attack and dominate other players, I studied the behavior of sharks, lions, and gorillas to gain a deeper understanding of the animal instincts and basic drives and needs that make people kill, cry, compete, and even love.

I wondered then if the lion's roar matters more than his bite. It's a metaphor, but its implications are real. Capitalism encourages competition and hard work, but cunning, intellect, and privilege get you in the ring. Privilege allows us to look upon certain evolutionary instincts with disdain, to act as if we're above violence, revenge, carnality, and chest thumping. Privilege allows us to preach reason and resort to it as a means of resolving problems. And for black men, to be successful, we have to neutralize white fears and anxieties with smiles and composure.

But the truth is that when another man barks at you, you instinctively feel the urge to bark back. When terrorists attack us, we strike back. When people stand before an audience, we may not say it or even realize it, but we're more inclined to like them, to give them a chance, when they're attractive and confident and appear to be among the fittest — those who seem the most capable and can survive in a competitive world. We try to instill humility and laud modesty, but deep down we appreciate the presence of power because it makes us feel secure. The truth is that we discourage fighting and yet most of us desire leaders who authorize killing others to protect us. The truth is that we act as if reason runs the world when in fact most of our lives are governed by the instincts, drives, and desires we try to suppress.

For every strong man, there is somewhere an even stronger man. I realized that the bite matters, but more often than not it's the lion's roar, the length and color of the mane — the handshake, the swagger, the demeanor, and one's presence — that are the deciding factors.

One of the best friends I made that summer at Stanford was a guy named Moe Katchen. We stayed in the same dorm and hung out often, at least a few times a week. We studied together, grabbed meals together, and explored Palo Alto and San Francisco together. Moe was an immensely likable guy — smart, empathetic, and cool, but also conscientious. We were tight, but after knowing each other for a couple of weeks we still hadn't discussed politics, and I heard from another classmate that he was a conservative.

Soon after, we were in the common room of our dorm just hanging out, and I started coming at Moe — playfully at first — about some of his conservative beliefs. "So," I asked him, "you're telling me that a flat tax is fair? That small government benefits the middle class?" Moe was a passionate but not bloodthirsty competitor. But he *was* a competitor. I, on the other hand, made no effort to conceal my taste for battle. I began going after Moe ruthlessly. My intent was to utterly dismantle his arguments. Moe stumbled, made some weak points, and wavered a bit. I stridently corrected him. The thing that impressed me, though, was that he never backed down. No matter how forcefully I came at him, he always bounced back.

The other people in the room listened with rapt attention. As our debate went on, our audience grew. Of course they loved the spectacle, and we were two popular guys with big personalities. After two hours, we had at least thirty or forty bystanders observing us as if they were watching a movie. I'd been waiting for something like this my whole life and loved every second of it. Moe wasn't in his element in quite the same way. He hadn't read as much as I had and got tripped up a few times by the evidence I presented. But he never relented. Over three hours, he put up a good fight and made it clear to me that he was a conservative for the right reasons, because of his principles. I respected that as well as his resilience.

Over the course of the summer, Moe and I ended up having three debates like this, and with each one, we only grew closer. I went at him with everything I had, and I admired the way he kept coming back. I hadn't found that in a friend or rival before — or since. After leaving Stanford, I missed Moe. He was the kind of friend I could debate with intensely and then chill with and talk to about almost anything. I made a few other friends like that at Stanford, and those connections made that summer special, one to remember.

Since doing forensics at Grosse Pointe Academy, I'd been interested in a career in public service. I knew that I cared very deeply about helping people and that I wanted to improve their quality of life by impacting different areas. But it wasn't until after leaving Bullis that I decided that I wanted to run for president one day. When I got to Stanford and peers asked me what I wanted to do, I shared that ambition with them, and many told me they believed I could win. It meant a great deal to know that they believed in me and my potential to make a positive difference in the world, and I began my time at Williams on the wings of their confidence.

CHAPTER 9
FRIDAY NIGHTS

Like Bullis, Williams offered me a generous financial aid package, but my family still had to come up with several thousand dollars a year for me to attend. The day I got my financial aid award, my dad's account balance was in the single digits. And he was already working three jobs. So our options were limited. He'd already pulled money out of his 401(k) early to make a down payment for my dental work, and my grandmother had already gotten a reverse mortgage to cover the remainder of my dental fees and repair the kitchen floor, which had caved in. We thought about taking out a loan, but my dad was still in debt, and his credit wasn't great. I thought about outside scholarships, but most deadlines had passed. And Peggy had already done so much for me and I was extremely grateful. I didn't want to ask her for more help. So paying the remainder of my Williams expenses would be a struggle.

I was aggravated. I knew Williams had a huge endowment. And while I appreciated the aid they offered, I thought it was problematic that most elite colleges with considerable endowments were frugal in granting aid to students from disadvantaged backgrounds. I understood the complexities. Colleges and universities needed a steady flow of donations to their endowments to meet their short- and long-term goals. To ensure a better future for their institutions, they have to grow their endowments. They also had to consider withdrawal rates. So most colleges could spend only 4 to 5 percent of their endowment per year. On top of that, some donations were onetime gifts; others were annual but specified for a particular purpose, so donations couldn't just be arbitrarily used to ease the burden on low-income students. Because of these factors and others — such as the state of the economy, inflation, and projected rates of return — simply handing out more money to students like me was hardly feasible. Yet I refused to accept the notion that wealthy institutions of higher education couldn't do better.

While it would be naive to suggest that a single blueprint could work for most colleges in America, there are questions that may inform useful approaches to solving the problem of rising college costs: How often does "demonstrated need" meet the actual need of the recipient and adequately account for financial circumstances that taxes and federal documentation do not inquire about? How are colleges prioritizing their range of institutional goals with the financial burdens placed on low-income students and their families? Are efforts to raise money sufficiently focused on financial aid? And does the unsettled idea of a tuition-relief fund with possible tax exemption necessarily have to detract from endowment donations? Or can the two amounts grow separately yet simultaneously? Answering these questions would not solve the problem but may help us think about how best to retool and refocus our efforts to address this pivotal issue.

Fortunately, my dad was able to find a small car in good shape for an affordable monthly rate. His plan was to start working as an Uber driver between jobs to make more money. There were hardly any hours left in the day for him to work more than he already was, but he managed, somehow, to do Uber a couple of hours a day. Once he noticed how lucrative Uber could be, he dropped the paper route and one valet shift a week to do Uber more often. Fortunately, this was enough to cover the part of my college tuition that wasn't covered by financial aid. The last car he had was in bad shape and too unreliable to drive far distances. But with his new car he would be able to drive me up to Williams.

On the way up to Williamstown, I told my dad about my mind-set going into the next four years: "I want to take my intellectual engagement to another level. If I adopt Kobe's polyphasic sleep schedule, I can read systematically across disciplines and cover more in the areas I value most. Conditions will be better, too, so I can go full throttle."

"Balance; don't you want balance?" he said.

"You always say that, but balance isn't what got me here. I have to push myself to my outermost limits. Good grades have never been my only goal. At Williams, I'll have access to every academic journal and periodical there is. No subscription fee. No paywall. No Internet issues. No space constraints. I'll be able to explore whatever I want, as much as I want, for as long as I want."

"You'll do what you want to do. But if you want that brain to work at its best, you have to sleep and eat. You don't feel it now, but wait till you're fifty."

"Right," I said. "So the plan is to brief three news outlets a day, read five academic journals a week, and a few magazines a month. If I aim for that, with course work and clubs, I'm sure I'll struggle to meet the mark. I can systematize the schedule, too, and increase each category by one each month if it's not difficult enough."

"Mm-hmm."

My dad always listened, but rarely with any genuine interest in my intellectual pursuits. Usually, he just nodded impassively. If he did comment, it was always on my lack of attention to things such as eating and sleeping on a regular schedule. Sometimes he also encouraged me to take on less. But I was going into my freshman year of college and was hell-bent on raising the bar. By then I knew my dad well enough to know that, with him, intellectual conversations were usually one-way. So I thought I might be able to gain some insight from him on drinking and dating, two aspects of college life that I was uncertain about.

My dad had gone to Ferrum College but dropped out toward the end of his second year. He'd told me some stories before, but I was curious to hear more about his experiences. Whenever I'd talked to my dad about girls and dating in the past, he painted a simple picture. At my age, he was a flirt — bold, carefree, and largely uninterested in deeper conversations and serious relationships. His approach was simple: "Go for it. All she can do is say no. If she does, there are plenty more fish in the sea."

From what I gathered, my dad had a solid success rate and a short memory. What may have seemed like an awkward moment or a fraction of self-doubt to most people was just an indication to move on to another girl for him. "So you've never thought twice about how to approach a girl or what to say?"

"I don't know; it just flows, and you get a vibe," he said, without giving it much thought.

"So you never really hesitated then?" I replied.

"Maybe back in middle school when I was shy."

"But not since then? Damn. You ever been played or gotten caught up?"

"Not that I can remember. I was usually seeing a few girls at a time until I met your mom."

"Did you care about them all?" I asked.

"Not really, not until things got serious

with your mom."

Unlike my dad, I was more deliberative and wanted to develop a connection with the girls I'd been interested in. For him, the main factor was physical attraction. Naturally, I looked for that first. But I also cared about other factors, such as a girl's personality, intelligence, values, and opinions. For those reasons, my dad had been a bit keener on hookup culture than I would be.

Our experiences with alcohol stood in even starker contrast. When he was younger, my dad drank a good bit. I knew that drinking was a big part of the typical college experience, and up to that point I'd never tried alcohol. James and I had opened a Bud Light at his house one time over the summer but decided not to drink it. I'd never been one to give in to peer pressure, but I wanted to be able to go out in college without worrying about how I'd handle alcohol. So I asked my dad if I could try some with him before he dropped me off at Williams.

Once we checked into our hotel room in Williamstown, we went out to a liquor store nearby and he bought a six-pack of Corona. When we got back, I tried one and hated the taste. But school didn't begin for another two days, and I wanted to see how much I could drink before I felt anything. So I finished it and grabbed another. Thirty minutes later, I was on my third. I asked my dad how much he thought I could drink and still be able to read analytically after going out.

"It depends," he said. "It's different for everyone. You don't have a lot of mass, so you may feel something after a few beers," he told me. "Over time, you build a tolerance. If you take a shot, it can hit you a little quicker."

By the time I'd gotten through my fourth bottle, I was buzzed. I was still myself, but more easygoing and relaxed. It wasn't a bad feeling, just peculiar. I felt loose and laid-back, as if I would be more likely to laugh at a bad joke. My dad got me a glass of water and told me to always hydrate afterward.

"You're gonna want to take it easy at first and avoid mixing drinks," he said. "If you're drinking hard alcohol, space it out. After shots, wait fifteen minutes and see how you feel. And always eat something before you drink."

The next morning, I woke up feeling a little groggy. I was still able to do everything normally, but I tried to write a letter to a friend at Stanford and realized I wasn't firing on all cylinders. That was enough for me to get a sense of my limits. Over the next four years, I wanted to be in optimal condition — to be more precise, efficient, focused, and sharper than ever. So I decided then that I would simply avoid drinking too much. To approach the life of the mind the way Kobe approached basketball, I had to be ready to perform at my best, whether that was at 3:00 a.m. or noon. Good grades had always been a goal of mine, but what motivated me the most was the prospect of reading more deeply and widely than I ever had before.

At freshman orientation (which Williams called First Days), students chose to join one of several groups to get to know classmates and learn about life at Williams. The group I joined was called Leading Minds, for students who were interested in becoming campus leaders. The first day, we went around introducing ourselves, and I volunteered to go first. I boldly laid out my goals for my time at Williams and the future. "I hope that over the next four years we can come together in cooperation for mutual enlightenment," I told the group, "and use all of our individual passions, talents, and energies to make the most of our time at Williams."

I brought that intention and intensity to every aspect of my life at Williams. Now that I was in college, I wanted to be a part of everything, to get to know everyone, and, most of all, to learn everything I could. When the time came to sign up for classes, I decided to take five classes instead of the usual four, including two infamously tough tutorial courses that most freshmen shy away from. But even that demanding course load wasn't enough.

I wanted to defy the limitations that stemmed from academia's natural tendency toward expertise and specialization. That meant exploring areas of knowledge I knew I'd never master. I had read a bit about the sociology of academia and the "publish or perish" impulse, so I understood why scholars specialized in particular fields of inquiry. One professor even told me that I would be better off in the long run focusing on one discipline and committing to it. I could certainly appreciate that perspective, especially as it came from a respected scholar. Like most people, I had certain abilities and areas in which I excelled. And my bread and butter had always been politics and philosophy. But I wanted to learn more about different kinds of subjects, even if I had no interest in pursuing a career in them. So while I picked my courses according to my level of interest in various subjects, I tried to read about everything from American architecture and the neuroscience of music to quantum tunneling and supersymmetry.

I'd read books written for popular audiences when I could access them through Williams's online library. But I focused mainly on academic journals. The first time I picked up a quantitative economics journal, the bulk of the math flew over my head. But after spending several hours over the next two days looking up some of the jargon and researching certain econometric concepts, I was able to make a bit more sense of the implications of the scholar's findings. For many who would never become an expert in those areas, reading journals like that one may seem like a waste of time. But my outlook was different. In my view, knowledge and understanding could only be gained by exploring new and unfamiliar terrain. So I believed in the value of expertise as strongly as I rejected the idea that any knowledge should be off-limits.

To be more efficient, I systematized my extracurricular reading routine. On average, I tried to explore a new topic every five to seven days. Given the range of topics I was curious about, my overarching goal was ambitious but practical: to get a sense of what the leading thinkers in various fields of interest were studying, why they were studying it, and if their research held any relevance to everyday life. To accomplish this, I would sometimes read academic journals in as many as twelve subject areas.

On several occasions, I was lucky to meet peers who were interested in the latest research in one of the subjects I was exploring. One of them was a guy named Dan. He lived in my dorm and was majoring in biochemistry. Dan was a science wiz, and I loved learning from him. We had some cool conversations about string theory, telomeres, and the cellular causes of aging. My talks with Dan helped me gain a better understanding of some of the practical implications of the scientific research I'd read. On most days, I did my extracurricular reading late at night, between midnight and 3:00 a.m. And on more than a few occasions, I didn't begin my class assignments until the morning of the day that they were due. But by this point I was used to juggling a heavy workload without missing deadlines or taking a hit on my grade point average.

There were things I liked about Williams: the well-maintained, bucolic campus; the welcoming, community vibe; and the generous dining and janitorial staff who went out of their way to be kind and gracious with their time. There were also things I loved about Williams: primarily the tutorial courses that consisted of two or three students who wrote papers and critiqued one another's work and one professor who gave each of us a lot of individual attention. These courses in particular gave me an opportunity to argue vigorously, ask tough questions, and dig into complicated subject areas. Even better, my own ideas were readily challenged, and I welcomed this. I was hungry for intelligent, invigorating debate and found tutorial sessions intellectually thrilling at their best.

One of my tutorial professors during freshman year was a brilliant black woman with a radical leftist bent. She was as sharp as a tack and absurdly well read. An influential black activist on campus had recommended the class, which was about the history of racial injustice, and when I heard that the professor had studied under Cornel West, I didn't hesitate to sign up.

In class, the professor pushed forward my analysis and understanding of gender in challenging and productive ways and taught me more about how black slaves found agency through subtle forms of resistance. But when discussing American history, she resisted acknowledging the contributions of the white men who were typically glorified, something I found problematic. American history includes a multitude of white men who, despite their many flaws, laid the foundation for the democratic ideals we all value and defend today. To deny their contributions because of their immoral decisions and hypocritical deeds was to throw out the baby with the bathwater. So I pushed, not too forcefully, and sometimes not even directly, but decidedly, for an account of American history that acknowledged the relevance of their contributions. These discussions were always respectful and friendly, but I was never successful in persuading her.

While I had several other terrific professors freshman year, the one who had the greatest impact on me was Professor David L. Smith, who taught an African American literature seminar. Professor Smith impressed me right away with his sharp clothes, refined sensibilities, and encyclopedic knowledge of history and culture. In class he consistently helped me make my own arguments stronger and deepened my perspective on the authors we read. Without sacrificing any nuance or complexity, he presented a range of sophisticated interpretations of the material we covered, compelling me to reconsider my own.

Outside class, Professor Smith became the most influential mentor and black male role model I've ever had. I spent hours at a time several days a week talking to him in his office about everything from literature to black feminism to what drives people, and he found a way to enhance my understanding of every topic we discussed.

Despite all the new intellectual stimulation, it took me a while to adjust to the laidback campus life at Williams. It is remote, with very limited accessibility, to say the least. Williams is located in the rural Berkshires of western Massachusetts, and our campus is in the middle of a tiny college town. Just to see certain movies, my friends and I would have to drive an hour to Albany, New York. I was always eager to do and experience and take in more, and the campus, while comfortable and scenic, felt almost claustrophobic at times.

But I didn't let constraints stop me from taking on all that Williams had to offer. In addition to my demanding course load, I regularly attended meetings of several campus clubs and ran for leadership positions in three of them, becoming the communications director of the Black Student Union as a freshman. I admired the passion and moral vision of many of the other BSU board members, and I was especially pleased by the fact that a woman named Sevonna Brown led the board and that there were more women in leadership roles than men. To me, that was a clear sign of progress, albeit a small one.

I enjoyed working with Sevonna and the other BSU board members. I shared their deep concern for the advancement of black people, though we had other differences of opinion. Namely, I wasn't as radical a leftist as most of them. Though I considered myself liberal and a progressive, I was more moderate. Most of the other board members spent a lot of time hanging out together in Rice House, where the BSU meetings were held. I liked them all personally, but it was important to me to spend time developing relationships with people in different social and student groups on campus.

I wanted it all, to be just as engaged socially as I was intellectually. In the dining hall, I often grabbed a meal with several students or groups of people a day, sometimes one after the other. Some groups talked about sports and whom they had hooked up with the weekend before. Others talked about politics and history paper assignments. I didn't care so much about the topic. I cared more about connecting with people and getting to know them better. So when I had something to contribute, I did. But I was also content to listen to what my new friends had to say and to learn more about them.

Going into my freshman year, I wanted to gain perspective by hearing other people's stories. I was curious to understand what motivated people from different cultural and socioeconomic backgrounds. And I also wanted to understand how they defined suffering, success, and failure, and what gave them joy. That first year, I also had high hopes of meeting the perfect girl. But reality settled in soon enough. I talked to a few girls but didn't find the right one for me. It was disappointing, but I told myself that it was only a matter of time.

The more meaningful relationships I formed my first year were with mentors like Professor Smith and two close friends, Cole and Walford. Cole was a basketball player who was one of the most consistent, supportive, loyal, and laid-back friends I'd had, the kind of guy who always wanted me around, understood when I had other things to do, and was happy to hang out and kick it even when he wanted to drink and I didn't. Walford was a close black friend on campus who was deeply religious but practical and open-minded and one of the coolest guys I've known. Walford was smart, funny, and sincere. He was one of very few people I spent time with at Williams or anywhere else whom I found I could just be myself around. He was the kind of guy who made you feel that, even if you didn't share them, your secrets were safe with him. If I could go back and do things over, I would like to have spent more time with Walford.

My roommate freshman year was a kid named Michael who was artistically gifted, easygoing, and funny. He could ease his way into any conversation with self-deprecation. Michael and I were living in the same room, but we came from drastically different backgrounds and had dissimilar demeanors and ambitions. He went out most weekend nights and came back tipsy. When he had a girl with him, I let him have the room and slept on the couch in the common room. Like some other people I met at Williams, Michael was going with the flow and sometimes just going through the motions.

Early in the year, I wanted to get to know Michael better. We were very different people; I wanted to understand how his experience at Williams differed from my own. What made him tick or feel some strong emotion? Late one night I was sitting at my desk reading while Michael lounged on his bed, strumming his guitar. "Are you happy here?" I asked him.

Michael shrugged and looked down at his guitar strings. "Happy enough, I guess," he said with a subdued smile.

"What does it mean to you?" I prodded, hoping to get to a more nuanced and truthful answer. "What do you want to get out of your time here?"

This time, Michael looked up at the ceiling, as if the answers were written up there. "I don't know," he told me. "I'm just trying to make my way through the crowd."

I paused, and though he was nothing at all like Michael, I thought about my dad. The best way to get through to him was to ask him about the things I knew he cared about and could relate to. In my dad's case, those things were basketball, girls, and maybe something on the news. With Michael, I figured it was girls, music, comedy, and art. So I switched gears and asked Michael about the elaborate cartoon images he'd drawn on his backpack. "What inspired those?"

Michael's face lit up. "Do you know Angel Boligán Corbo?" he asked. I shook my head no. "He's a Cuban cartoonist; he's amazing. His work really captures Cuba's dark history, but it's also hilarious." I eyed Michael's backpack with a new appreciation. "I wanted to skip college completely and try to get my own art career off the ground," he told me. "But after high school you go to college. It's just what you do, right?"

I chose my words carefully. To me, going to college wasn't merely the status quo. It was a hard-won means to what would inevitably, no matter where it led, be an even harder-won end. But everything about Michael — particularly his unhurried, mellow demeanor — spoke to an untroubled, uncomplicated life, so it made sense to me that he was moving forward merely because no one else was standing still. After our conversation that night, I felt restless and missed my friends like Moe back at Stanford, whom I had a lot more in common with. After Michael went to sleep I stayed up rereading poems by Robert Frost and e. e. cummings until he got up to go to class in the morning.

Unlike most of my peers, I still didn't enjoy drinking. But I also didn't like letting people down, so it could be stressful at times. Most Friday nights, I'd get texts from several people inviting me to pregame with them at their dorm before going to a party. I didn't really want to drink, but I did want to experience different social scenes on campus, and the few times I'd been out before coming to Williams, I had fun.

One Friday night I was pregaming with some football guys who'd go hard three nights a week. One of them tossed me a beer and I said, "Good look." But I only said that because I wanted to fit in. A week later, I found myself in a somewhat similar situation. But this time the crowd was different, and I wasn't the only guy who didn't want to drink. So I talked with a few guys while other people played beer pong. Before long, I'd shared with them my ambition to one day run for president. A few days later, one of the guys I'd been talking to that night named Eric found me on campus and asked me to hang out and grab a meal with him.

We sat down together in the dining hall, and Eric told me that he'd decided that he wanted to run for president of South Korea. His family had moved to the States from South Korea when Eric was in fifth grade. I asked when he'd landed on this goal. "At the party last week when you were talking about running," he told me. I didn't say it then, but I was touched. We talked about the global economy and Eric's desire to one day unite the two Koreas under democratic leadership.

Right away, I appreciated Eric's intellect, thoughtfulness, and self-discipline. As we became closer throughout the year, I saw that he was very focused, hardworking, and loyal, and he won more of my admiration and respect. We became great friends in part because we were both so highly motivated, but also because we both had an abiding interest in using our talents and resources to help others.

After Eric and I finished our meal and he went to the library, I went over to sit with some friends from the football team.

"Aye, you a forehead-having-ass nigga."

"You a face-ass nigga, Larry the lobster big-body-looking-ass nigga."

"Nappy-ass nigga, got pubic hairs on your chin. Boy, you so ugly you made your momma cry when you came out."

I was used to it by now, the way some of my black friends on the football team at Williams roasted one another. The dynamic was interesting because even though I wasn't on the team, we were boys. Yet I never really got roasted. At most, one of them would jokingly say, "Damn, nigga, can you wear shorter shorts next time?"

Before I came to Williams, Peggy had bought me some clothes from stores I didn't have the money to shop at, so I had a few pairs of J.Crew shorts and some other preppy-looking athletic clothing. Most of my black friends on the football team usually wore athletic apparel: Dri-FIT shirts, with joggers, Nikes, and the like. I hung out with them at least once a week. And they joned on one another all the time. Sometimes it would go on forever.

A lot of the jokes were hilariously stupid, but some were clever, and some of the guys were quick on their feet. Others were less inclined to go back and forth and would usually get annoyed or leave after a while. Battles could get intense, but ultimately it was friendly. When I first started hanging out with the guys, it was uncomfortable sometimes. Everyone would be joning on one another energetically, and I'd be in the awkward position of laughing but not too hard because I didn't feel comfortable roasting anybody myself and didn't want to give someone a reason to flame me, either. But it would have been too weird to sit there with a straight face while everyone else was engaged.

I'd played on inner-city basketball teams and gone to summer camps in Detroit with guys who joned on one another. I'd seen it at Bullis playing football, too. I'd even seen fights break out over roasting at the Anacostia Metro station. But I hardly engaged in it myself. I lacked the confidence and didn't feel the same impulse to participate, perhaps because I had other friends who didn't habitually flame one another.

I also avoided engaging sometimes because I could sense that beneath their facade, most of the guys I'd been around resented the feeling of being excessively targeted. I'd never heard anyone say that, but I could read their body language. The culture of joning had often made it more difficult for me to fit in, especially at first, but I'd always found my way around it. Yet I'd never really thought about why joning of the sort I'd experienced was far more common among black people, particularly among young black men.

Was it a way of bonding and belonging? A way of flexing and surviving? A way of emulating hip-hop culture and being cool? Or was it a combination of those elements and other psychosocial factors? I'm not sure if there is one clear-cut explanation, but I know that with roasting often comes an uneven mix of love, laughter, vulnerability, resentment, and power. Sometimes it's playful. Sometimes it's fraternal. Other times it's defensive, contested, and barbed with sharp edges. At Williams, I fit in with the guys enough to dap them up, grab dinner, and go out on the weekend. I fit in enough to be in the group message but was still known as the guy who may turn down a pregame to reread a book by a dead white man.

During the fall of my freshman year, I heard that a group on campus called Uncomfortable Learning was inviting Harvard Law School professor and author Randall Kennedy to come to speak about his book *Nigger.* A group of three Williams students had started Uncomfortable Learning the year before. It was a guest lecture series meant to facilitate further discussion of topics that they felt were presented and supported one-sidedly on campus.

I held Randall Kennedy in high regard and had already read his work, so I was looking forward to meeting him. During the weeks before his visit, I reread each of his books and contemplated what questions I should ask him.

In anticipation of Kennedy's talk, I also

spent time thinking about how my view on the use of the word *nigger* had evolved over time. During high school, I'd generally thought that with art being one of the few exceptions, only black people should use the word. My reasoning was simple: because the word *nigger* had been used to oppress black people, black people should be able to dictate its use. To me, that made using the word *nigga* as a term of endearment perfectly fine.

I also thought that it was obnoxious and inconsiderate of white people to ask for permission to use the word. The very idea of their asking annoyed me. As I saw it, a white person could not be genuinely sympathetic toward black suffering without understanding the need for them to refrain from using the word *nigger.* Yet since I'd started going to GPA in fourth grade, I'd been asked by white friends for permission to use the word many times.

Despite what I actually thought, I rarely, if ever, objected to white peers using the word around me. I knew that I was only being asked for permission in the first place because that peer sensed that saying *nigger* might bother me. Why give them that power? Why let them think that saying a single word in front of me could ruin my day or make me want to cry or start a fight?

My mom had taught me that it was important to make an effort to be in command of your own emotions because revealing anger, or even irritation, would give some people the satisfaction of knowing how to get under your skin. As a kid, I sometimes found it difficult to heed this advice. But as I grew older, it influenced my thinking on the word *nigger* and other offensive speech.

By the time I was at Williams, I largely agreed with Kennedy: I would not be friends with any white person who used the word *unreflectively.* But I didn't think there was anything particularly wrong with white people using the word. I believed context mattered and that they should be mindful of potential consequences. In the classroom and in other, similar settings, I thought it reasonable to establish speech restrictions conducive to learning and productive dialogue. But aside from that, it is up to individuals whether to be judicious in how they express themselves.

On the day of the event, I spoke to Kennedy before his talk, and he told me to keep in touch. When it was time for the question-and-answer session, I was prepared. I asked Kennedy a question that required him to either explain or reconcile seemingly contradictory statements written in two of his books: How could he be okay with white people using the word *nigger* when permitting their use of the word could also encourage the very "casual and unreflective reliance on racial distinctions" that he challenges?

After the event, the president of Uncomfortable Learning, Keith, came up to me and introduced himself. "I liked your question," he told me. "You seem like the kind of guy who should be a part of our group." I met up with Keith soon after at the Williams snack bar. We talked about the future of Uncomfortable Learning and what speakers I was interested in. Keith was a senior, and he wanted me to get involved then so that I could help run Uncomfortable Learning when he graduated. I appreciated Keith's kindness and intellectual curiosity, and I liked what the group stood for.

I dived right in, taking over advertising for the speakers who were lined up for the rest of that year. At the time, attendance at the lectures was averaging about forty to sixty students, and I saw that Uncomfortable Learning had more potential. If I was going to get involved, I wanted to transform it into something that would make waves and positively affect campus culture in a big way and push students to open their minds and broaden their perspectives.

I soon sensed that some of the other BSU board members felt I was spreading myself too thin and wanted the BSU to be my number one priority. They noticed that I hardly ever hung out with them at Rice House because I was too busy doing other things, and this was problematic for some of them. I wanted to be equally engaged with many groups at that time. Focusing exclusively on the BSU was not an option. So, out of respect for the level of commitment that I thought the board deserved, I resigned.

Going home soon after I stepped down from the BSU board for winter break was for once a welcome respite. I missed my family and had been so busy and focused at Williams that I hardly had time to text my dad once a week. When I arrived, things at home were relatively calm; with one less mouth to feed, my dad's finances were in slightly better shape. It felt good to come back as a college student, and it was a little easier to appreciate being home after being away. Besides reading and writing, I spent time watching movies with my uncle Lee and hanging out with Nicole. On my way back to Williams, I thought about the kind of life I wanted to be able to give my own family one day and how my dad once told me that the upside of all his sacrifices was that Nicole and I would be able to do more for our kids.

Shortly after I got back to campus, I was having dinner with a few other students. We were discussing how racism and sexism operated in America. Many of their arguments were clear, strong, and compelling. The upshot thus far had been that patriarchy and racism were so deeply entrenched in America that mechanisms of the existing political system were inadequate to achieve racial justice. While I agreed with much of their analysis of the issues we face, I was less convinced by that conclusion precisely because it depended on there being a consensus about what a just world should look like.

We'd also been talking for an hour and had discussed injustice only from the perspectives of radical black activists and literary figures such as June Jordan, Audre Lorde, Angela Davis, and bell hooks. I'd learned a great deal from each of those thinkers, but I was unsatisfied with discussing race from only a far-left perspective. And I firmly believed in the potential of

America's political system to effect positive change. So I asked them what they thought of Condoleezza Rice.

They all looked vexed by the question.

"She's an imperialist, who has chosen to forget where she came from." The others nodded, and chimed in briefly. "She thinks rich white people actually like her."

I could tell from the snarky comments and dismissive looks on their faces that they had no interest in discussing the ideas or attitudes of black conservatives. In most cases, I would have pushed back or argued more forcefully in favor of thinking about race in a more nuanced way, but I'd been on campus for only a few months and I'd largely anticipated their reactions. I knew that challenging them would have led to a series of unpleasant remarks and possibly a falling-out, so I changed the subject to Williams professors they recommend I take courses with, since they were sophomores and juniors.

I'd been in many situations like this where the people I was talking to, whether students or professors, wanted to talk only about people, ideas, and initiatives that they agreed with. More often than not, I'd quibble, if not argue. Sometimes, I'd argue aggressively, even taking stances I completely disagreed with. But I always judged the situation first. Could an intellectual argument with this person damage our relationship? Hurt their feelings? Did they seem equipped or eager to debate, or more interested in agreeable conversation?

Plus, I didn't feel the urge to argue all the time; no one does. But there were times when I was frustrated by the refusal of many liberal students and professors to engage with conservative ideas. I was also frustrated by those, usually on the right, who actively resisted talking about issues such as racism and sexism. So the frustration went both ways, though it was often easier to get my conservative peers to reflect on more liberal ideas than the other way around. This didn't surprise me, though, mainly because most of the far-left students unwilling to engage with conservative ideas were minorities who often took controversial issues personally, owing to difficult, sometimes traumatic, life experiences. Still, I picked my battles carefully through most of my freshman year because I wanted to establish myself first and forge relationships with people before going against the grain in a more concentrated way.

CHAPTER 10
SHOULDER TO THE WHEEL

The summer after freshman year, I attended the Summer Writing Institute at Yale University. On balance, my time at Yale paled in comparison to my time at Stanford. That was because the monthlong writing conference at Yale was mostly for middle-aged authors looking to advance their careers. Yet Yale was still an awesome experience. And, sure enough, I was determined to make the most of my time there. I reached out via e-mail to some thirty professors whose work I had read and met with as many of them as I could. Due to their limited availability and conflicting schedules, I was only able to meet with about a dozen scholars in the law school, humanities, and social science departments. But each of the conversations I had helped me gain a deeper understanding of what it meant to be an academic and a scholar.

Whereas in the past I would have asked

the professors questions mainly about their ideas, my goal in each of these meetings was to learn more about their methods, approaches, and styles of reasoning. I wanted to grasp the methodological differences between various disciplines and how scholars with an expertise in one field engaged with other areas that shed light on the issues that interested them.

When I wasn't in a writing workshop or meeting with a professor, I was enjoying New Haven and hanging out with a girl I'd met at the bookstore named Allegra. Within a few days of our meeting, Allegra and I were doing everything together: eating meals, going to the gym, exploring the city, watching Netflix, and going out to watch the NBA Finals at the bars nearby. Sometimes we even did our writing assignments together in my room, since I had a single and she had a roommate.

Allegra was gorgeous, fun, and easy to talk to, but I tried to spend time with her without building expectations for anything serious. I have fond memories of the time we shared, even though she was a bit more forward and free-spirited than I was. We still talk from time to time, but regular conversations petered out shortly after we left. I met another girl later that summer, and we saw each other casually for a while, but I was still disappointed by the fact that I hadn't yet found the right girl to pursue a serious relationship with.

When the Yale program ended, I spent some time at home in DC before heading back to Williams. At home, I considered everything I had accomplished during freshman year: establishing myself on campus as someone committed to engaging with serious issues, broadening my intellectual horizons, developing friendships, and earning the respect of my classmates. Then I thought about what I wanted to accomplish in the coming year: to challenge people and their understanding — and therefore my own — of complex issues by pushing the boundaries of what it meant to play devil's advocate.

At Stanford, I had enjoyed and learned quite a bit from invigorating, often intense debate. There were still many complicated issues that I wanted to consider from different viewpoints, but at Williams, most of the people I interacted with were more interested in finding common ground and treading lightly than in going head-to-head. This attitude made the campus feel like a welcoming community and helped me make friends and feel grounded there, but now it was time to put my shoulder to the wheel and begin the work that would define my time at Williams.

Over the next two weeks, I wrote two articles, "Everything That Offends Black People Is Not Racist" and "Blaming White Racism for Violence," which were published in *The Undergraduate Times* and *The Washington Times,* respectively. In these articles, I stated some demonstrable facts, but I also argued against many of my own beliefs, taking on a conservative "All Lives Matter" approach to racism and police brutality.

I wasn't hoping to offend people, but I was looking to provoke them. I knew that if I told people ahead of time that I was writing from an alternate perspective as an intellectual exercise, they wouldn't bother to argue with me. It was only by committing to these arguments that I could hopefully inspire people to speak out, therefore giving me a chance to debate.

Of course, I was well aware of the risks involved in doing this. Namely, that if I had one ounce of political success in the future, people would come back to those articles and use them against me. But I was undeterred. I weighed those risks with the potential rewards. To me, those gains would be an opportunity to engage in illuminating debate and to find out what would happen if I went against the grain and people thought I believed what I wrote instead of the same notions as most of my peers on campus.

When the articles came out, shortly before the beginning of my sophomore year, many people, especially my friends in the black community at Williams, were confused, angry, and hurt. I received comments and messages ranging from "What happened to you? Did you get abducted?" to simply "Zach, no!" When people commented, I almost always responded by giving them my phone number and saying, "Give me a call; I'd love to talk about it more," but they rarely did. My close friends — my boys like Eric, Walford, and Cole — had my back. They knew who I really was and felt no need to argue with me. But others simply shut me out.

I was back on campus just a few days later. Few people actually brought up the articles, but there was a slight tension in the air that permeated many of my interactions. When I saw my friends from the basketball and football teams, they treated me no differently, and many even expressed their support because they knew me well enough to know what I was all about. Members of the

305

BSU and other student activists, on the other hand, felt betrayed. Some still dapped me up or said hi, but with many, there was an elephant in the room, a slight hesitance behind their eyes as they spoke to me. When people brought up the articles directly, I asked what they thought of them. Some said it was brave, while others resented what I'd written. No matter how they responded, I always made an effort to engage respectfully without demeaning myself by sustaining a conversation with people who sought only to insult me.

Within weeks of school starting, the *Williams Alternative* republished my article from *The Undergraduate Times*. This time, it really struck a nerve, because these controversial views were being introduced in a place that many of my classmates thought of as their home. I knew they would be upset, and I was ready for it. I felt confident enough in my opinions that I could hold my own and talk about them respectfully, even with people who vehemently disagreed with me. When I walked into the cafeteria the day it was published, almost every head turned in my direction. People were paying attention, and I felt determined to do something useful with that.

Eric and I had decided to be roommates

that year. We were a good match; Eric was the only person I knew who worked as hard as me. When we were in our room together, we were either working or having intense conversations about politics, literature, academics, or life experiences. Most nights, we'd stay up late working and then go to the snack bar together after midnight.

Early in the year, I met with Chris and Jake, the two remaining presidents of Uncomfortable Learning. Keith had graduated the previous spring, though he remained a great friend and loyal adviser. Chris and Jake confirmed what Keith had told me the year before — they wanted me to gradually accept more responsibilities throughout the year and ultimately take over the group when they graduated. We also discussed the speakers list for the coming year. The first speaker who was scheduled to come was John Christy, a climate scientist at the University of Alabama in Huntsville who has dismissed the scientific consensus on climate change and was considered a climate change denier. It was a successful event, and several students engaged productively with Christy, pushing back against his arguments that the changes in the earth's climate weren't caused by humans or reason for alarm.

I was encouraged to see this level of engagement and eager to start publicizing the next speaker we had scheduled, Suzanne Venker, an author and self-described anti-feminist. We knew going in that Venker would be different from Christy or any of the speakers who had come to campus the previous year. Venker's views that feminism was a war against men, that marriages are healthier when women work less and stay at home more, and that wives should be subordinate to their husbands were so counter to the women's equality and empowerment that many of the women and men on campus believed in and were fighting so hard to achieve.

Knowing this, Chris and Jake were concerned about being associated with the event. They were both junior advisers and didn't want to risk jeopardizing their relationships with the freshmen they advised, so I volunteered to put up posters and set up an invitation on Facebook for the event.

Within minutes of my posting the event, my phone lit up with texts, comments, and other messages. One after another, comments appeared on the event's page. There were dozens — eventually hundreds — but none of them was positive. "It's nice to know that Zach Wood, a former leader of the BSU, is actually a men's activist," one read. Another said, "Zach Wood, you're a filthy dirty misogynist." I was called a sellout and a traitor and told that I needed Jesus. But there was one lengthy comment posted by a well-known campus activist that I thought captured the sentiments of the most radical factions on campus, who most strongly opposed Venker's visit. It read:

When you bring a misogynistic, white supremacist men's rights activist to campus in the name of "dialogue" and "the other side," you are not only causing actual mental, social, psychological, and physical harm to students, but you are also — paying — for the continued dispersal of violent ideologies that kill our black and brown (trans) femme sisters. You are giving those who spout violence the money that so desperately needs to be funneled to black and brown (trans) femme communities, to people who are leading the revolution, who are surviving in the streets, who are dying in the streets. Know, you are dipping your hands in their blood, Zach Wood.

Protests were quickly planned, as well as a

feminist counter-event. I was excited to see all this activity and hoped it would result in productive conversations, but Chris and Jake were alarmed by the backlash and decided to cancel the event. It was majority rule, so I had no choice but to stand by their decision. But as soon as the decision to cancel the invitation was made, I didn't waste any time. By the end of that night, I had written a response, which I published in the *Williams Alternative.*

In my piece, I said that at Williams, learning should begin with confronting challenging ideas, and I explained that while tens of millions of Americans espoused Venker's views, I was not one of them. I believed that her arguments deserved trenchant criticism but that to challenge her intellectually and critique her arguments, we had to first understand them. Engaging with Venker's ideas was not an ideological endorsement. Whether we agreed with her or not, we all could learn something from Venker's work.

I wrote that those who protested viewed this event through a lens of motivated ignorance and suggested that students make an effort, individually, to understand the very best counterarguments on the issues that they cared about most. Intellectual integrity, I argued, does not necessarily entail changing one's mind. Rather, intellectual integrity consists of the willingness to be self-critical and think as hard as one can about counterarguments out of the understanding that each of us can and should try to learn from those with whom we vociferously disagree.

Over the next few days, everyone on campus was talking about that article. Fifty students announced they were getting together to write a response, which I eagerly awaited. I had approached that piece, like everything else, with intention. Yes, I was aggravated by the character attacks, but I didn't waste time disputing them; rather, I resolved to prove that although her speech was canceled, I was not afraid of Venker's views, nor did I agree with them. In fact, I was more than willing to take them on.

It was frustrating to me that by effectively shutting down her speech, campus activists had provided fodder for the conservatives who mockingly call progressives liberal snowflakes. In my life, I had felt fear, and I refused to feel that way again. There were no words, beliefs, or philosophies that I would allow to frighten or intimidate me. I wanted to confront and disprove the depiction of liberals and progressives as timid or weak or, worse, unable to defend their own positions, and it rankled me that by canceling the event, we had ended up playing right into their hands.

Sure enough, when Venker wrote about the cancellation on Fox News, she said, "The students who took issue with my appearance are as sensitive as their feminist leaders, who are notorious for cowering in the face of opposition. And I understand why: their arguments are weak. And weak arguments can't hold up to scrutiny."

My piece in response to the cancellation took Venker's visit from a campus controversy to a nationwide scandal. I began receiving calls from editors at national newspapers asking for a quote, an interview, or a written response. CNN, *The Washington Post,* and many other outlets covered the controversy surrounding the decision to cancel Venker's speech as part of a bigger conversation about free speech and whether colleges and universities should protect students' feelings by offering a "safe space" that keeps out oppositional voices.

Even my mom called me when she saw what I'd written. "You have handled yourself like a man," she said. "That's how I raised you to be." We hadn't talked much since my visit during my senior year of high school, but now we began to speak on the phone

once every couple of weeks for thirty minutes to an hour at a time. My mom supported everything I was doing, read every
interview I gave and article I wrote, and
provided me with some valuable nuggets of
wisdom about how to approach different
people in light of this controversy.

By then, we had a tacit understanding that
the only way we could move forward with
any type of relationship was to look forward,
not back, and essentially pretend that nothing bad had ever happened. So that's what
we did. I sensed from our talks that she was
more stable and better able to restrain her
emotions than she had been previously, but
we never spoke about the past. Instead, we
focused our conversations on how I could
answer certain interview questions, and she
helped me develop a core competency in
conducting effective media relations.

When I wasn't doing interviews, writing
articles — which I did for a national outlet
every month going forward — or focusing
on my course work, I took my own advice
and sat down with students one-on-one and
in groups to understand their perspectives.
It was important to me to demonstrate that
Uncomfortable Learning was about more
than winning an argument; it was also about
understanding what mattered to other

people and why. So, as part of my own uncomfortable learning, I focused on trying to engage with various people who disagreed with what I was doing.

The tenor of these conversations varied, based on whom I was talking to. If someone came at me aggressively, I hit right back. But if people just wanted to talk and express how someone like Venker made them feel, I did my best to listen attentively so that I could understand as fully as possible and then let them know which factors of their analysis and experience resonated with me.

Many of those students remained unconvinced, but I felt confident that they left our discussions knowing that I was not simply evil or opportunistic, and that instead I had valid reasons for what I was doing — even if they were reasons they personally disagreed with. I learned from those conversations, too, that some of my critics weren't merely as hypersensitive and intolerant as I'd assumed. Some of them had a more sophisticated and nuanced argument. They believed that these issues had been conclusively decided upon and were no longer up for debate, and that belaboring the issue was unnecessarily hurtful, bordering on abusive. Though I understood their perspective better, they did little to sway me. The way I saw it, if millions of people still believed in what someone was saying, it was essential to engage with their argument and directly take it on.

After the uproar over Venker, Chris and Jake decided to step down as presidents of Uncomfortable Learning and left me to run it by myself. That was fine with me. Chris and Jake had been the ones to cancel Venker's speech, so I reinvited her the next day. Unfortunately, she had already published her speech online, so she declined the invitation.

Uncomfortable Learning already had the next speaker planned — KC Johnson, a professor of history at Brooklyn College and the CUNY Graduate Center and the co-author of *The Campus Rape Frenzy: The Attack on Due Process at America's Universities.* Johnson had drawn criticism for his beliefs that campus policies unfairly presume guilt when a student is accused of rape or sexual assault. Chris, one of the former co-presidents of Uncomfortable Learning, had originally invited KC and wanted to rejoin now that things had settled down. I welcomed him back and set about preparing for the event.

I had some sense of which students on campus would be most upset with Johnson's visit, so I tried to preempt some of the potential uproar by seeking out certain individuals beforehand so that I could explain my position one-on-one. I told them, "I'm not convinced by many of the things KC Johnson has to say about campus sexual assault policies, and I'm sure you disagree with him, too. That's why I'm hoping you'll come to the event and take him to task. That's what this is all about. I'm not asking you to come and listen to him so he can change your mind. I'm asking you to come and counterargue as hard as you can."

When we announced the event, I got nothing but radio silence. There was no uproar. But I still wasn't sure how the event itself would go. Would there be protests? Silence? Maybe no one would show up at all. As I stood near the podium in front of the lecture hall, chatting with Johnson before the lecture began, I saw several students I'd spoken to and a few from various activist groups on campus enter the room and take their seats near the front. There were students from BSU, the Williams College Feminist Collective, and other minority student groups. By the time the lecture began, the room was mostly full. And I was happy with the turnout.

Johnson's lecture went smoothly. He was

316

professional, polished, and well prepared. Then came the time for the question-and-answer session. More than a dozen people in the audience challenged him, asking smart, pointed, well-crafted questions. Among the most pointed was a question about how his analysis accounts for the pervasiveness of misogyny and sexism as is clearly manifested in STEM fields.

Johnson was shrewd and perspicacious and answered each question thoughtfully, ramifying and clarifying his answers when necessary. He never folded under the pressure, but students in the audience made him work. Many of his claims were duly challenged, and weaker areas of his argument were clearly exposed. In the end, it was a great debate, with ideas being exchanged, criticized, and complicated in a fruitful way. It was a beautiful thing to see, and I leaned against the door at the back of the room thinking, *This is exactly what we need.*

If the story ended here, it would seem as though I'd done the impossible and successfully transformed campus culture to be more tolerant and open to free discussion. But I wanted to take on other, more controversial topics, too, so I embraced the challenge of bringing them to the forefront of campus debates.

CHAPTER 11
EVOLUTION

That winter of 2015, all anyone around the country could talk about was the upcoming presidential election. Williams was no exception. We discussed it in class, in the cafeteria, and even at parties.

I was particularly interested to observe and better understand the role that race had played in the campaigns and in the media coverage. It was such a sensitive and complex topic, and I saw that some of the people who cared about race relations in this country the most also thought they understood the subject so well that it was no longer worth discussing. But my life had taught me that confidence, like aggression, could betray my intelligence if I wasn't cognizant.

In some sense, the issue of race was a lot like evolution. Everyone had some idea of how it works. But when was the last time I'd met someone who could explain the evolution of the human eye? There were a lot of smart people in the world who tried to explain things that they'd never seen or experienced. It was like talking about constellations without understanding the intricacies of how a telescope worked. I saw nothing inherently wrong with this, but I tried to be mindful of the difference between relying on reason and imagination.

I wanted to take on the issue of race the same way I tackled every issue that was of personal or intellectual interest to me. And that was by hearing as many different perspectives on it as possible to develop a nuanced understanding of why people thought and felt about it the way they did. In my mind, this was the natural next step for Uncomfortable Learning — to invite a speaker with controversial views on race so that we could confront racism head-on.

After the successful event with KC Johnson, who had been last on his docket of speakers, Chris had hopped back off the board of Uncomfortable Learning. Now I was running it on my own with the help of a few peers who had joined after Johnson's event. They saw that I had faced a lot of criticism and chose to join the club because they believed in its mission and the impact I was trying to make on campus. I enjoyed having them on board and was glad that students had taken an interest in UL.

I remembered hearing about John Derbyshire, a pop-math author and longtime columnist for *National Review*. He'd been fired a few years before for some writings that were widely believed to be racist. In particular, Derbyshire published the script of a "talk" that he recommended white and Asian parents have with their kids about what made black people different from them and the threats they posed to their own children's safety. He claimed that 5 percent of black people were "ferociously hostile" to whites and argued that if white and Asian parents warned their children not to stay long or live in predominantly black communities, it might end up saving their lives.

When I decided to invite John Derbyshire to speak at an Uncomfortable Learning event, I understood that backlash was inevitable. As a liberal black Democrat, I knew that I'd be seen as a traitor or a sellout at worst, and as a closeted conservative at best. But I believed in the work that I was doing, and I was ready to take on my critics and fight back effectively to demonstrate that racial controversies could be intellectually engaged in meaningful ways.

After everything I'd experienced that year,

my ambitions were clearer to me than ever before. With the kind of change I wanted to make in the world, I could not back down or withdraw. There would always be resistance to what I wanted to do, so I had to learn how to work productively with people of various ideological stripes. And the best way to do this, I saw, was by interacting with them and trying to get a sense of who they were beyond the scope of our respective opinions on controversial issues.

When Randall Kennedy came to speak at Williams the year before, I had tried to find points we disagreed on so that I could understand him better, even though we shared many of the same views. Now I wanted to do the same thing with Derbyshire. I disagreed with him vehemently on most issues, but did we share any commonalities or points of intersection? If so, what were they? How could I use that knowledge to inform the ways in which I engaged with politics and controversy?

I was aware that every major reform ever passed in this country had been grounded in a deep knowledge of people's circumstances and therefore why they needed realities to change. I didn't expect that I would be able to persuade someone like Derbyshire, no matter how much information I might have presented to him. But that wasn't the point. Debating him would better enable me to expose the flaws in his argument, to argue and defend my own position, and, perhaps, if I did that effectively enough, to change the mind of someone in the audience. On many issues, there are always people in the middle who are relatively undecided. I saw intellectual argumentation as a means of persuading those people and of encouraging them to reflect on visions and viewpoints that might be less familiar to them, given their particular backgrounds and experiences.

For so long, I'd been striving to gain knowledge about topics I was less familiar with. And now I wanted to push myself even more to immerse myself in the complexities of what my opponents thought and felt so that I could use them in service of my own goals. I saw it somewhat like a game of chess. If all I knew going into a challenge was that I detested someone's views or that I wanted to win, I'd be starting the game with inadequate preparation. But if I knew my opponent well enough to confidently conjecture his moves and lines of reasoning, I could act astutely and respond effectively.

My studies had taught me that there were many ways to create change. Protests and activism were important and meaningful ways of applying social pressure. But I also felt that when we began to fear our ability to bring people to some truth, there was a problem. Yes, there were times when it was sensible to dismiss rank racism and sexism and homophobia and say that a person had not earned a particular platform; yet we still have to acknowledge that person's individual right to free speech. Engaging with some manner of ideas I felt were obnoxious — as some of Derbyshire's were — was about believing that they were wrong, and if they were wrong, then that wrongness could be made apparent.

With all that in mind, I posted the invitation to the event. The backlash came swiftly and furiously. People were hurt and confused, but mostly they were angry. Within moments, I was inundated with messages, texts, and comments reading, "Who knew you could be black and a white supremacist?" and, "Zach Wood may look black, but as far as I'm concerned he's white."

None of this fazed me, but one afternoon I found a small slip of paper that had been slid underneath my door. "Your blood will be in the leaves," it read, next to a hand-drawn picture of a tree, with leaves scattered beneath it.

The next day, a blocked number called my cell phone and left a message making implicit threats. I even received a suspicious package that was screened by the Office of Student Life before I could open it. It was from a federal prison and contained a strange letter from a prison inmate.

When I talked to my dad about all this, he said, "You just keep going at it, huh?" He was right. Again, I tried to walk the walk. I sat down to talk to a roomful of black campus activists at Rice House to gain a better understanding of the range of opinions on the issue. The conversation lasted for more than two hours.

"You know what I'm about," I told them. "You know who I am. What I'm doing with Uncomfortable Learning is trying to use this as a platform to speak to a number of different issues. We can take them on and see them not just as affronts to our humanity but also as opportunities to win. I want you guys to win," I assured them, "and I want to win with you. But we gain nothing from running and hiding from controversy or pretending that we can censor people we don't want to hear from."

Most of the people in the room expressed their dissenting opinions cordially; many were insightful and informative. Toward the end of the discussion, however, emotions rose to the surface. This issue was personal and cut deeply for them. They felt that bringing Derbyshire to campus was an attack on their humanity and black identity. "You may be an intellectual looking for a good debate, Zach," one person said. "But this isn't about an argument to me; this is personal. You need to bring a Black Panther or BLM activist and make these white people uncomfortable."

I understood how painful this issue could be for many black students on campus. Surely, I had my own grievances about racism. And I cared deeply about increasing black success and achievement. But the answer wasn't to shut down and withdraw. Real change could only come from engaging and getting outside myself by trying to put myself in the shoes of another person whose ideas I could not fathom.

The students in the room were understandably angry, and I appreciated their willingness to sit down and talk with me, but they didn't really seem interested in sustaining an argument with me. It felt like they wanted to persuade me, to welcome me back into the fold whenever, as they saw it, I came to my senses. I was not able to persuade them, and vice versa. But I listened to everything they had to say and spent some time over the next few days reflecting on how my decisions would impact their experience at Williams.

There were some people on campus, though, who supported what I was doing. Cole, in particular, and several other friends on the basketball, football, and lacrosse teams supported my efforts. Eric also had my back to the extent that he was personally offended by the character attacks that were made against me. I appreciated Eric's loyalty and Walford's, too. Walford was someone who rarely posted on social media, but when I took on my detractors in the comments section on Facebook, he was there, liking my posts and encouraging me in person to "keep pushing." He told me, "I wouldn't do what you're doing, and I'm not even sure I agree with it, but I know what kind of guy you are, and you have my support, man."

But my efforts did little good. When my phone rang just two days after I'd posted the invitation and I saw that it was the Williams administration calling, I knew what was about to happen. I didn't answer, letting it go to voice mail. Adam Falk, the president of Williams, left a message for me saying that he couldn't allow Derbyshire to speak on campus. He said that he'd be willing to speak with me about his decision (after it had been made), but I saw no need. Minutes later, he sent a campus-wide message to students saying he was canceling the event.

He'd exercised his power, and now it was time for me to exercise mine. The only power I possessed, besides knowledge, was the written word. I wrote an article responding to Falk's decision, calling it "not merely injudicious, but undemocratic, irresponsible, and, frankly, pathetic." The Associated Press interviewed me about the article, which had the whole campus talking and led to dozens of interview requests. I was gratified to see that most of the media coverage was critical of Falk's decision to cancel the event, even if some questioned my motives for inviting Derbyshire in the first place.

Even some of my close friends and mentors saw my invitation to John Derbyshire as a personal betrayal. "Zach, you're consorting with demons," one mentor told me. "You're adding your name to a long list of conservatives who've turned their backs on their own race." I disagreed. How was seeking to come to a more nuanced understanding of race and racism a way of turning my back? The way I saw it, those who refused to discuss issues of race or only discussed them one-sidedly were the ones with their backs turned. I took a stand and did so imperfectly, but I did my best. I was confident in my position, yet it was still painful to lose the respect of mentors and peers.

Fortunately, there were many who supported me. A few weeks after Derbyshire's event was canceled, NPR ran a debate series called Intelligence Squared about free speech on college campuses. It was live-streamed from Yale University. Wendy Kaminer, a lawyer, writer, and civil libertarian, was arguing on the side of free speech. She had interviewed me prior to the debate and told me that she planned to reference my story in her argument.

On the night of the debate, I told some of my friends on the basketball and football teams at dinner that I'd be mentioned, and they said they wanted to watch it with me. I knew that many of them didn't really care about the issue of free speech on college campuses the way I did, and it was a Friday night when they surely had other things they'd rather be doing. But they showed up anyway and watched intently, asking questions and commenting on various points being made. It meant a lot.

From across the common room, Cole tossed me a beer. I still wasn't a big drinker, but throughout sophomore year I'd gotten more comfortable with the party scene on campus. I was responsible and always observed my limits, but I did go out a bit more and have a good time.

As the debate went on, I was disappointed that I wasn't mentioned. But when it was time for Kaminer's closing argument, she began by saying, "We have just been talking about intolerance for speakers with dissenting views. A few days ago, I spoke to Zachary Wood . . ."

My friends and I were hyped. She told my whole story — the canceled events and the backlash, even the implicit threats. She also spoke about how disturbing it was that some black students on campus had talked about me in slave dialect and liked Facebook comments referencing slavery, such as, "We need the oil and switch to deal with him in this midnight hour."

Kaminer's entire argument concluded with my story, and when the vote came in from the live audience, 66 percent were on her side and only 25 percent against, with 9 percent undecided. I wasn't satisfied, but I was happy, if only for a few minutes. My friends live-tweeted and Snapchatted the entire closing statement; it felt good to get the win, and even better to have their support.

On my way to the bathroom soon after, I ran into a guy in my dorm named Bryce. "What up, Zach. Yo, what was everybody talking about on Snapchat earlier?"

"Big debate on free speech," I told him. "One of the debaters talked about me in her closing statement."

"That's sick, dude. Huge for the program."

That was the first time I'd actually talked to Bryce. He was a specimen, virile and irreverent. He walked around with a royal air, the kind of confidence that had no memory or fear of vulnerability. I envied that about him. Bryce wasn't the best student, but that didn't matter. He was tall, white, rich, and good-looking. He played on the football team, dated the most popular girl in the sophomore class, and took enough hits from his gravity bong to live in the clouds.

I would love to tell you that I only wanted to be myself, that, by this point in my life, I felt that what I had to offer was good enough. But I didn't. I didn't want to live like Bryce or act like him. I wanted to worry as little as he did. I wanted to feel as secure about my manhood as Bryce felt about his.

I wanted to measure up to my mother's unrealistic ideal of a real man.

Yet I'd also learned to reject grand theory, the idea that any one view or understanding of the world could capture reality in all its complexity. Humanity of course entails commonality and some degree of empathy. But what it means to be a man or manly differs for different people. Scholars often discuss this idea of hedging our bets in terms of arguments about nature and nurture and cultural relativism or the limits of drawing inferences from representative samples. But the main takeaway, as I've come to see it, is that context matters. What it means to be right or wrong, happy or sad, masculine or feminine, admirable or detestable, and so on depends on more factors than any of us can fully ascertain at once. Theory is useful because it helps us dissect, compartmentalize, and better understand facets of reality in intelligible ways. But every theory is imperfect. When they're strong, theories and the evidence used to support them offer a sense of cohesion, clarity, and cogency that helps us make sense of our lives. But no one argument or view adequately explains every aspect of any issue. With that perspective, I still couldn't deny my mother's influence, but I tried to think less about my mom's opinions and more about how I could honor my own sense of what it meant to be a person of value and strong character.

I was determined to see things to fruition. If I couldn't get Derbyshire to campus, perhaps there was a way to bring someone else who shared similar views but whom Falk could not shut down without being accused of blatant censorship. This led me to Charles Murray, whom I'd heard about years before. Murray was a political scientist, columnist, and author best known for the book *The Bell Curve,* in which he uses the genetic component of intelligence to argue against social welfare programs. Murray was controversial, but he was a scholar held in high regard by many. It would be nearly impossible to argue against the value of debating someone like Murray, whose beliefs were echoed in the current presidential campaign and certainly not being censored there.

When I posted the invitation to the event, the comments came. The criticisms came. The outrage came. But this time the tone was somewhat more subdued, as if my harshest critics had realized that I wasn't backing down and they had to find another way to counter my actions.

Directly before the event, the Williams College Debating Union invited Joseph L. Graves Jr., an evolutionary and nano-biologist and historian of science, to deliver a speech called "Race, Genomics, and Intelligence: Slight Return," which countered Murray's ideas about the connection between intelligence and race. Many of the students who attended Graves's speech stayed to hear Murray, using what they'd learned to push back against his claims. I relished the idea of this. It was precisely the type of debate I had been wishing for since arriving at Williams. Plus, this meant that the auditorium was packed when Murray arrived to give his talk.

In his speech, Murray emphasized the importance of genetics, claiming, "Nothing has zero heritability." Then he warned the students in the audience to "buckle up," knowing that what he was about to say would be met with skepticism and hostility. His argument was that genetic knowledge should be incorporated into the social sciences, stating that this would lead to a rediscovery of human nature and human diversity that would prove the equality premise was wrong. People, he said, "are not equal in their latent abilities and characteristics."

"I just don't believe that there is any college professor who seriously believes that all the kids in his classes, if they had had identical upbringings and environments, would have identical academic ability," Murray said. "I don't think anybody believes that."

In the front row of the auditorium, I sat forward in my seat. I hadn't expected for anything Murray said to resonate with me, but his statement made me think about the connections in my own life between my upbringing, environments, and academic ability. Yes, genetics clearly played a role. My mom, despite her flaws, was brilliant. She'd taught me so many invaluable things, particularly about human nature. And though my dad didn't share my intellectual drive, his own intelligence lay in the perceptive and discerning way he viewed the world.

My upbringing and my environments growing up had provided seemingly endless challenges at times but also opportunities. Would I have developed the same thirst for knowledge if I didn't have access to the books and magazines in Lola and Papa's basement, if my mom hadn't drilled into me the importance of being presentable and well-spoken? Or even if I hadn't been motivated at times to lose myself and escape from my reality in the world of a book?

As Murray finished his speech and began fielding questions, I thought about the fact that I couldn't separate one from the whole. There was no way to tease apart where each separate element of my character came from — my intellectual drive, my ambition, and my desire to connect with others and understand them so that I could one day do whatever was in my power to help them. These things were a combination of the gifts, curses, and blessings I'd received from my parents, and so was I.

I saw my mom that summer for the second time since I had left her home six years before. She asked me to come up to Michigan to visit, but I said that I preferred for her to come to DC. Though she didn't say it explicitly, I sensed from talking to her throughout the year that she understood she'd done some things to make me feel uncomfortable during our last visit and did not want to repeat those mistakes. So I felt optimistic about our visit and more comfortable seeing her on my own turf. I knew that if she said or did something that was out of line, I could leave.

After checking in to her hotel, she picked me up at home. Over the next few days, we explored DC and went to the Martin Luther

King Jr. Memorial, the Washington Monument, and the Lincoln Memorial. I showed her around the Bullis campus and Potomac, Maryland. And we went shopping. She bought me more clothes than I'd ever had at one time in my life. It felt good to know that I wouldn't have to worry about having enough clothes for the foreseeable future.

Throughout those four days, we talked. And our conversations were for once as meaningful as they were normal. She spoke to me and treated me differently than she had in the past. She was appropriately affectionate, gave me space, and treated me like an adult. For the first day or two she was there, I braced myself for something to go wrong, but when it didn't, I began to relax and actually enjoy our time together.

It was a good visit, the best yet by far, and I held on to the hope that things between us would continue to improve. It was that hope, that faith in humanity and one's power to change and learn and grow, that had kept me going. Without it, I would have been lost years before in a storm of confusion and anger. But now the storm had dissipated, and I left that visit with my mom determined to keep pushing forward to do and accomplish more than before — not just to help students with a paper or expose them to uncomfortable views but to find a way to make a positive fundamental difference in their lives. I wasn't there yet, but I wouldn't rest until I arrived.

EPILOGUE

I haven't seen my mom since she visited me
in DC last summer, but we've talked regularly over the last year. Talking about the
past is too difficult, so we mostly act as if it
never happened. It's surprising sometimes
how naturally we try to tread carefully
around certain subjects and avoid pushing
each other's buttons. Usually our conversations are about my goals, ideas, and role
models; my understanding of the world and
people around me; and the discrepancies
between things as they are and things as
they should be. Despite small bumps in the
road, she's been there for me over the last
year as an adviser, a loyal fan, and in some
cases even a confidante. When I think about
our relationship now, it's easier for me to
see it in a more positive light, to recognize
the knowledge and insight I've gained from
her, to appreciate her contributions to the
man I am today and the man I want to

become in the future.

It's been almost two years since I became a controversial figure for advocating free speech and intellectual engagement on college campuses, no matter how provocative or offensive the subject matter or speaker. To some, free speech has become a defining issue for my generation. In the last few years, too many speakers have been disinvited by college administrators. To promote inclusion, various measures — often contested by activists — have been taken to discourage and constrain free debate at universities across the country. Like any other complicated issue, free speech doesn't exist in a vacuum. It intersects with issues of racism, sexism, and bigotry. Rarely, if ever, are there easy answers to questions regarding entrenched moral and political disputes.

But I believe that making headway with issues of expression and inclusion in America will require patience, persistence, and a demonstrated willingness to thoughtfully engage from all sides. It should be acknowledged that some conservatives have used arguments about free speech and intellectual freedom to attack liberals and dismissively characterize them as narrow-minded, intolerant, and oversensitive. In response, several liberal commentators have hit back, suggesting that some conservatives only champion free speech now because their views are less prominent in American institutions of higher education.

The dispute between the liberals and conservatives over free speech has only intensified in light of recent legislation passed in North Carolina, Tennessee, and several other states that requires college administrations at public universities to punish students for repeatedly disrupting speakers. While the legislation passed in Tennessee is fairly comprehensive and thoughtful and sets an important precedent, there are pros and cons to the bills passed in each of these states. Although some of the legislation takes a step in the right direction, it is critical that the focus of educators and administrators remain on ways of enhancing education as opposed to merely enacting punishment.

Since becoming the president of Uncomfortable Learning, I've had the opportunity to attend many conferences focused on issues of free speech and intellectual diversity on campus. At these conferences, I've had the pleasure of meeting and talking with some of the most distinguished First Amendment scholars in America. Though

I've learned a great deal from many of them, I was most intrigued by the arguments of Stanley Fish. After we attended a conference together, I made a point of staying in touch.

Over dinner recently, we discussed a range of issues from cultural appropriation and hate speech to the pitfalls of ideological approaches to problem solving. His argument about free speech was one of the most compelling I'd heard and the only one that challenged me to see the free-speech debate in an entirely different light. Put simply, Stanley argued that free speech doesn't exist and that we should be happy about that. Rather, the real value to fight for in higher education is free inquiry for faculty, not students. In his view, censorship happens all the time in the form of grading, tenure review, academic publication, and who gets called on in class. In each of these cases, speech is suppressed and, at times, literally discouraged, based on subjective criteria. To Stanley, the purpose of a university is the pursuit of truth and the creation of new knowledge. All that requires is the freedom of faculty to interrogate whatever they choose and design their courses as they see fit.

To the surprise of some of my supporters,

I hardly disagree with any of that. My contention is more a matter of context and practicality. As I see it, within the bounds of the current debate, supporting free speech on college campuses is a way of promoting intellectual growth and sparking debate, a way of resisting the impulse to become insular and tribalistic in our engagement with controversial topics. Whether free speech ever literally exists, then, is somewhat beside the point. What matters more to me is that people make an effort to use dialogue and disagreement to test their assumptions, to build understanding, and hopefully to cultivate greater empathy.

Over the last few years, I've learned that common ground is more likely to be found when I approach people in good faith and do my best to give them the benefit of the doubt. More often than not, that approach feels like a tall order when I consider the degree to which human beings are naturally self-interested. So I fall short of that goal and many others more often than I'd like to admit. In his memoir, *My Life,* Bill Clinton quotes at length from an essay he wrote in high school about self-knowledge. Though I've written papers with similar sentiments, I refer more often to his words when the going gets tough:

I am a living paradox — deeply religious, yet not as convinced of my exact beliefs as I ought to be; wanting responsibility yet shirking it; loving the truth but often times giving way to falsity. . . . I detest selfishness, but see it in the mirror every day. . . . I, in my attempts to be honest, will not be the hypocrite I hate.

I refer to this passage because I can relate to it but also because it is comforting if not encouraging to remember that someone as capable and successful as Bill Clinton experienced similar feelings of self-doubt. Whether we express it or keep it to ourselves, I think all of us share a common complexity of being that is far deeper than the rhetoric surrounding any controversial topic. I love to debate, and sometimes I try to spark it. But understanding people — what motivates them and gives them joy, what empowers them and inspires them — is indispensable to being the kind of leader and change agent I aspire to become.

I believe that change and progress are often incremental. And sometimes it's frustrating, having a vision, moral or political, that must be revised or adapted to be feasible in the context of the real world. I often find myself trying to reconcile the need for pragmatism with the value of conviction, the importance of consistency with the power of open-mindedness. But when I reflect on these tensions and others that don't lend themselves to satisfying resolutions, I think about the aspects of my identity and personal history that shape my engagement with issues I care about and discuss with others. In light of all that I don't know, I am reminded of what I know for sure: I'll always have something to gain from the perspectives of others.

ACKNOWLEDGMENTS

I am immensely grateful to the many people without whom this book could not have been written. I am particularly indebted to Jodi Lipper, who devoted more than five months of her life to helping me shape this book and craft it into an engaging story. Without her insight, patience, and dedication, this manuscript would have never seen the light of day. To Brandi Bowles, thank you for giving me a chance — for believing in me and in the potential of my story to make a positive difference. Without your guidance and encouragement, this book would still be just a proposal. To Jessica Renheim, I simply couldn't have asked for a better editor. Your judgment and feel have greatly improved the quality and readability of the manuscript. Throughout this process, and particularly when I've faced challenges in dealing with difficult personal issues within these pages, you've been kind, helpful, dependable, and understanding. Thank you, Jess, for being an absolute pleasure to work with.

I also wish to thank my book team at Dutton — specifically Christine Ball, John Parsley, Amanda Walker, Carrie Swetonic, Elina Vaysbeyn, Abby Endler, Chris Lin, Jill Schwartzman, Yuki Hirose, Alice Dalrymple, and Marya Pasciuto for their generous efforts and gracious support. To be sure, this book is a testament to their gifts and talents.

To my family, none of this would be possible without your enduring love and support. And no amount of gratitude may equal the credit you deserve for whatever good has come out of my life. Despite the challenges of our relationship, I would not be where I am today without my mother. For giving me life, love, and the strength to overcome any obstacle, words are inadequate to express the depth of my gratitude. When I think about the kind of man I aspire to be, I feel blessed to have an outstanding father. Dad, I cannot thank you enough for all the sacrifices you've made to give me a better life. Thank you for teaching me the value of hard work, and thank you for being a man I could always admire.

To Grandma, thank you for caring for me in all the ways a grandmother should and more. Your love has been keenly and consistently felt. To Lola, thank you for teaching me how to read and encouraging me to test my assumptions and ask questions that challenge my understanding of the world. Some of my happiest memories are of moments we spent together when I was young. To Peggy Cooper Cafritz, since I have known you, you have been there for me every time I've needed you. I love you dearly and am extremely grateful for all that you've done for me. Because of you, some of my childhood dreams are now among my most memorable experiences.

When I decided to write this book, I knew it would entail sharing some of the most difficult aspects of my life. Without the enthusiastic support and encouragement of loyal and loving friends, I would not have been able to complete the task. Alex Sun, I simply can't thank you enough for being the best best friend I could ask for. To Parker Smith, thank you for being there, homie, for helping me early on to think through various technical challenges of this process, and for being a great friend. To Chirag Manyapu, thank you for supporting all my efforts and for coming through promptly when I've called on you. When the going has gotten tough, it's been reassuring and meant a great deal to have you in my corner.

To Cole Teal, thanks for showing love, bro, and for being the kind of friend I could trust and confide in. Whether it's an article or an interview or a TED talk, you're usually one of the first to check it out and offer positive feedback. Years from now, when I look back on my college experience, the time we've spent together will surely be among my fondest memories. To Luke Higgins, you're one of the most thoughtful guys I know. Throughout this process, you've been one of few people I could talk to with zero fear of judgment. Thank you for listening, remembering, and pointing out the positive side of the balance sheet. To Chongsuk (Eric), I've relished the many probing conversations we've had about life. You're one of the most disciplined, hardworking people I know, and being around you has motivated me to sustain my efforts, especially when I've felt like I was on my last legs.

I owe special thanks to Drew Peisch. Our conversations over the years have been extremely rewarding. You've hit me with tough questions and cogent arguments and helped me refine my ideas and clarify my thoughts on various issues. In addition, our conversations have demonstrated time and again that great friendships can transcend political differences; that great friends learn from and appreciate the differences between them. I also want to thank other friends who've been there for me. Austin Thomas, we've become close friends over the last couple of years. Thanks for being there to give me your input — whether it be on intellectual, social, or personal matters. Kicking it with you in New York and at Williams gave me something to look forward to when my mind was consumed with the implications of sharing my life story.

A special word of thanks goes to Kyrien Edwards for giving me great advice. Key, thanks for keeping it real and being generous with your time. Joe Sageman, you've been a loyal and supportive friend since we met my freshman year playing football. Thanks for the good times, bro — and thank you for reminding me to consider the evidence. Because of you, I've developed a better sense of what it means to be pragmatic. Thank you also to Jaelon Moaney, Tyler Patterson, Adam Regensburg, and Matt O'Connor for leading by example and encouraging me to be who I am. Whenever I'm around you guys, I'm reminded of the little things each of us can do to make a positive difference.

To Mr. Lapadot and Ms. Jerome, thank you for making school something I could look forward to and be excited about every day. Our world is a better place because of educators like you.

I am deeply indebted to two exceptional mentors who read all or part of the book and made helpful suggestions for editing. To David L. Smith, your impact on me goes far beyond useful comments on early drafts of the manuscript. I would like to thank you for being the first person to read it, but, more importantly, for taking the time to help me work through my biggest concerns. To Reginald Dwayne Betts, thank you for answering my endless questions about what writing this book may entail. And thank you for helping me see that I could embrace vulnerability without shame. Without your advice, responsiveness, and ongoing support, my capacity to complete this book would have diminished.

To George E. Marcus and Steven Gerrard, I offer my heartfelt thanks for consistently supporting my intellectual efforts. I am extremely fortunate to have had you both as educators and advisers. To Kathryn Tabb, thank you for helping me deal with some of the book's more delicate content. I'd often leave our conversations feeling better about everything. To Amy Cuddy, thank you for your presence; you inspire me to reach ever further.

Finally, I'd like to give special thanks to Reanne Young for believing in me when I doubted my ability to drop everything and start all over again. At a time when my life was filled with anxiety and uncertainty, you helped me find the inner strength necessary to keep moving forward.

ABOUT THE AUTHOR

Zachary R. Wood is a Robert L. Bartley Fellow at *The Wall Street Journal* and a class of 2018 graduate of Williams College, where he served as president of Uncomfortable Learning, a student group that sparked national controversy by inviting provocative speakers to campus. His recent work has appeared in *The Washington Post*, *The Nation*, *Inside Higher Ed*, *Times Higher Education*, and *SLAM* magazine. A Washington, DC, native, Wood currently resides in New York City.